The Garden Trellis

DESIGNS TO BUILD AND
VINES TO CULTIVATE

The Garden Trellis

DESIGNS TO BUILD AND VINES TO CULTIVATE

Written and Illustrated by
FERRIS COOK

Artisan New York

Designer: Jennifer S. Hong
Production director: Hope Koturo

A NOTE ABOUT THE ENDPAPERS
The design is adapted from a piece of fabric that my friend
Judith Ogus found at the Salvation Army. Framed with it was a frag-
ment of a letter that read: "It's a piece of an apron that was brought
from England many many years ago soon after the close of the war
with France when Napoleon I was taken at Waterloo and the pattern
consists of the word P‑E‑A‑C‑E as you will see by looking. This
pattern was invented as a memorial of the close of the war. It is a
great curiosity." I wanted to use it in association with the garden,
because it's the best place I know to find peace. — FC

Published in 1996 by Artisan,
a division of Workman Publishing Company, Inc.
708 Broadway
New York, NY 10003‑9555

Library of Congress Cataloging‑in‑Publication Data

Cook, Ferris.
The garden trellis : designs to build and vines to cultivate /
written and illustrated by Ferris Cook.
Includes bibliographical references (p. 91) and index.
ISBN 1‑885183‑18‑6
1. Trellises.   2. Ornamental climbing plants.   3. Gardening.
I. Title.
SB473.5.C67   1996   96‑21060
635.9'74—dc20   CIP

Printed in Singapore
10 9 8 7 6 5 4 3
Third Printing

In memory of Peter A. Cook
(1928 – 1996)

contents

tangling with vines

When I started gardening ten years ago I felt an unusual peace. I vowed to myself that my garden would never be a place where I felt fear. Probably not everyone makes this a prerequisite to gardening, but living and working in New York City, I found a new weekend tranquility two hours north in Ulster County. I didn't want to worry about anything . . . no master plan . . . no back-breaking work . . . no poisonous shortcuts . . . only one plant at a time and nothing fancy. This was a place to have fun and watch the seasons. Before long, I became fascinated with vines.

I love vines simply because they grow so tall and I remain so short. The idea of growing a plant that climbs on its own made me a little bit nervous, but I liked the idea that vines take care of themselves. Of course, all kinds of plants—tall or short, big or small—should have a place in the garden. The joy of seeing an eight-foot sunflower is akin to that of studying the tiny, velvety, black flowers of *Viola* 'Bowles Black' on your hands and knees. But I couldn't keep my mind off vines and I started buying small vine seedlings.

While noticing huge poison ivy and grapevines in the woods, I thought about the story of Jack and his beanstalk. Then I remembered the talking and walking plants that run through *Alice in Wonderland* and the "Day of the Triffids." But contemplating the murderous plants in the "Little Shop of Horrors," I wondered if rampant, predaceous vines weren't the stuff of fiction and if my little vine garden might just strangle the house. My suspicions were confirmed when I found an article entitled "A Long Vine" in the *American Agriculturalist* from 1864, which reported a volunteer citrus-melon vine measuring 381 feet and producing a little over 41 pounds of fruit. The article goes on to say that "Mr. Warner gives a very complete and interesting measurement of all the different parts of the vine, for which we have not room." Some things are too big even to describe.

The truth is, I've had more frights in the garden than I've ever had in the city. A flat tire on the Triborough Bridge is terrifying until you see the bridge crew come to the rescue. And it is frightening to have your pocket picked in a revolving door, but other people notice these crimes and offer to help. But when you're in the garden, a puff of cigarette smoke or the more malodorous burning of plastic garbage is fundamentally more disturbing because you don't expect it. After all, it's paradise. Once there was a sudden bang! when the next-door neighbor blew a snake in half with a shotgun to alleviate the fears of his wife. Unfortunately, he didn't realize that I was quietly weeding in my garden, only a few feet away. Even the pears seem dangerous when bluejays and flickers cast unripe fruit to the ground by our parked car, the way little pieces of ornament come off buildings in New York City. Some of the real physical dangers are a bit remote: Lyme disease in deer country, skin cancer from too much sun, rabid raccoons and porcupines and bats, and the stings of hornets and bees. But a mysterious snake, probably just a harmless black snake, snoozing in the ceiling of the barn is a reminder that the force of nature is out of your control.

While I'm amused by the real adventures in the country, I can be a victim of the paranoid wanderings of my imagination. When I vacuum up the paper wasps, spiders, bat guano, and other commonplaces during spring cleaning, I'm not sure that we won't have a remake of "The Fly" in my vacuum bag or puppy-size insects when I go to the basement to do the wash. You must remember that for most of the year I'm a city dweller. To stand alone at 3 A. M. in the backyard while my family is asleep inside can take courage. One time I carried my puppy Stella out for a midnight walk and heard the approach of a thundering stampede. Just the deer, no doubt, but my heart pounded and I rushed indoors. Still, even after all my successes with vines I worry about them. Will the porcelain berry cover the woodpile the way kudzu has shrouded parts of Mississippi? Could the honeysuckle strangle the dogwood? And will the wisteria remove the front porch?

Soon after beginning my garden I bought some trellises at a yard sale—I couldn't resist them. Their simple lines promised an instant vine garden. But these old trellises spent years in the barn because I wasn't sure what I wanted to plant.

Eventually I put one trellis on the east side of a former outhouse, now my tool shed, to support a red rose that was already growing there. This rose trailed into the grass, making it difficult to mow the lawn without getting scratched. I planted a purple Jackman clematis nearby, and the flowers bloomed at the same time, making a flare by the Fourth of July. It was a patriotic scene, the white trellis, carmine red roses, and not quite blue clematis—a combination that became associated with the holiday. But I resented the red rose because it wasn't fragrant and I cut it down. As it recovered in the course of the next two years, I realized how eager I was to see it again. After years of working in an office I've learned the benefit of the absence of perfumes, so why ostracize a fragrance-free rose? What mattered was visual delight, not aroma. The successful combination of the rose and the clematis led me to put up another trellis on the south side of the tool shed. There I planted *Lonicera × brownii* 'Dropmore Scarlet.' When the honeysuckle no longer enhances the little house, or it impedes access to the tools, the clippers take revenge. And the honeysuckle keeps on blooming. Some vines, including this one, have more presence with their lanky arms intact, but they don't mind clipping any more than your hair does.

I searched for new vines and found more than I imagined. Some are relatively new in the trade, but most of them have been in garden literature for a hundred years or longer. Charles Darwin studied many of the climbing plants that were new to me but still easy to obtain. He marveled at their speed of twining and found that the common hop (*Humulus lupulus*) made a complete revolution in search of a support stick in 2 hours 8 minutes, and *Akebia quinata* did the same in 1 hour 38 minutes. While Darwin timed the revolutions of many vines, he also varied the size of supports to see what the maximum circumference each plant could reach around.

It's fun to study the direction vines spiral up a support. Do they twine clockwise or counterclockwise? I first thought that a vine that twined to the left in the southern hemisphere would twine to the right in the northern hemisphere. Wrong! The way a vine twines has nothing to do with the way the world turns. The direction a particular vine twines is fixed in its genes, an inherited and predictable trait, like the arrangement of its flower parts. Alphonse Karr described how some vines twine in *A Tour Round My Garden* from 1854:

> *The convolvulus, which opens its beautiful bells of all colours in the morning a little before day; the scarlet-runner, with its brilliant flowers, which climbs to the tops of trees; the Wistaria, with its blue clusters, which covers my house—form their spirals from left to right; whilst the honeysuckle, my dear honeysuckle, as well as the hop, turn about supporting trees from right to left, and that always without exception.*

As far as the left to right, or right to left, you have to imagine that you're a small creature in the garden, something nice like a toad, looking up a tree or pole. Is the vine growing up clockwise or counterclockwise? Remember, it will be the opposite if you look down from above the plant. In my reading about vines, I've found more than my own confusion on this. And, of course, I'm looking for clarity and not confusion in the garden.

I knew that the wisteria and spring- and fall-blooming clematis climbing on my front porch would overtake any small trellis, but other vines that were new to me needed a chance to grow before being assigned to a garden of their own. My climbing hydrangea (*Hydrangea petiolaris*) had to be planted at the foot of a tree, and other gigantic vines that I thought were unsuitable for my trellises, but which I'm trying to include elsewhere, are: silver lace vine (*Polygonum aubertii*), magnolia vine (*Schisandra chinensis*), and Dutchman's pipe (*Aristolochia durior*). How to grow these monsters—or where to grow them while allowing them to have room to be their giant selves—is a subject for another book.

My experiments took off with the addition of annual vines. Suddenly I had more vines than I could accommodate. They grew on poles and fences, through shrubs, and around young trees. I kept a notebook and made drawings—trying to figure out which ones I'd want to grow on my few favorite trellises.

This book describes my search for the right vines to grow in my garden and tells how to build some small trellises to grow them on. The first plants I profile are perennial vines that can grow in my area, which is in Zone 5. I began with honey-suckles, roses, and clematis and discovered actinidia, ampelopsis, and akebia along the way. Trumpet vine and the perennial pea are common and had to be tried, as well as the evergreens euonymus and firethorn.

The second group of vines includes those that are treated as annuals in the north. Some are perennials in their tropical homes, but if they flower the first year from seed they are considered with the annuals, even though in milder areas they may be grown, with some winter protection, as tender perennials. I grew many species of *Ipomoea*: morning glories, moonflowers, cypress vine, cardinal climber, sweet potato vine, and Spanish flag. I also planted nasturtiums and their cousin canary bird vine, as well as scarlet runner beans, purple hyacinth bean, black-eyed Susan vine, cathedral bells, sweet peas, and love-in-a-puff. I won't dwell on my failures, but I do want to try again the purple bell vine (*Rhodochiton atrosanguineum*), Japanese hop (*Humulus japonicus*), and chickabiddy (*Asarina scandens*).

Whether you're in the city or country, I hope that you will find here at least one trellis and one vine to create a perfect vertical garden.

plant profiles

honeysuckle

Lonicera (lon-ɪss-er-uh)

The honeysuckle family includes a large group of mostly woody shrubs, including *Viburnum* and *Weigela*, native to temperate regions. All of the honeysuckles, *Lonicera*, are named after a German naturalist, Adam Lonitzer, who lived from 1528 to 1586.

LONICERA × BROWNII 'DROPMORE SCARLET'

If I were to have only one trellis, I'd probably plant a honeysuckle. This is because one of my first successes was *Lonicera × brownii* (BROW-ne-i) 'Dropmore Scarlet.' Sometimes *L. × brownii* is listed under the name of Brown's honeysuckle and other times as the scarlet trumpet honeysuckle. Either way, 'Dropmore Scarlet' is a recent cultivar of a cross developed before 1853 of the trumpet, or coral, honeysuckle, *L. sempervirens* (sem-per-vɪ-renz, meaning "evergreen"), and the hairy honeysuckle, *L. hirsuta* (hir-su-ta, meaning "covered with hair" or "prickly"). Both of these species are native to the southeastern states; *L. sempervirens* was planted by George Washington at Mount Vernon. The leaves are oval and sometimes joined to form a disk; where the winters are mild, they are evergreen. All of the honeysuckles are twiners, and they all twine counterclockwise.

I chose *L. × brownii* 'Dropmore Scarlet' because it's recommended for northern gardens. Developed by Dr. Frank Skinner in Dropmore, Manitoba, it is hardy in Zones 3–9 and grows 6 to 8 feet high. In my garden the vine grew quickly and easily, blooming in early June and flowering throughout the first summer. It continues to thrive with a prolific blooming in June followed by a sporadic blooming until the frost, all the while attracting hummingbirds. Its most distinctive difference from my other honeysuckles is its joined leaf—almost round—from which the flower emerges.

Because there are several similar-looking honeysuckles, it's important to remember both their species and cultivar names. I'm misled by the name 'Dropmore Scarlet'—it seems as if 'Dropmore' should refer to falling petals instead of a place in Manitoba, and 'Scarlet' should refer to a bright red color, although according to some sources this cultivar varies from orange to red. My flowers are a dull red—not bright—on the outside and a very bright yellow-orange—not scarlet—on the inside. Despite the misnomer, I'm fond of the plant because it reminds me of my friend Scarlett. After all, I have a 'Norman' spiraea for my brother and a 'Sarah' mountain laurel for my sister. There's also Geum 'Mrs. Bradshaw,' not named for my childhood piano teacher, but none- theless planted in her memory.

LONICERA × HECKROTTII

For fragrance, I like the everblooming or goldflame honeysuckle, Lonicera × heckrottii (hek-ROT-ee-i). (It is often listed as L. × h. 'Goldflame.') Its origin is not certain, but it's thought to be a cross between L. sempervirens and L. × ameri- cana, introduced before 1895. In the day- time and at night its sweetness fills the surrounding garden, and, as long as there is new growth, it con- tinues to bloom. Oddly, although most descrip- tions of the flowers mention little or no scent, I find my plant's pleasing and pronounced. The buds are carmine, but when they open, the flowers quickly become pink with a purple tinge outside and yellow within. This vine blooms steadily all summer, and the individual flowers are bigger and more flamboyant than those of trumpet honeysuckles. I'd say it's my favorite. The goldflame is reported hardy in Zones 4–9.

LONICERA SEMPERVIRENS 'ALABAMA CRIMSON'

The red honeysuckle that I love is *Lonicera sempervirens* 'Alabama Crimson' (Zones 4–9). The blue-green leaves contrast beautifully with the vivid red trumpets in layers of six-flowered pinwheels.

The flowers are not fragrant, provoking Alice Coats to write in her authoritative book on the history of shrubs that "a honeysuckle without scent is like a man without a shadow." In the sun it grows quickly and will become 10 to 20 feet tall.

A couple of very fragrant honeysuckles are cultivars of the native European woodbine, *Lonicera periclymenum* (per-ree-KLI-men-um). Its name comes from the Greek for honeysuckle, *periklumenon*. It grows 10 to 20 feet tall in Zones 5–8 and produces red fruit. This is the honeysuckle mentioned frequently in Shakespeare.

In *Much Ado About Nothing*, III.i, for example, Hero schemes to have his cousin Beatrice overhear a conversation while concealed beneath the honeysuckle:

And bid her steal into the pleached bower
Where honey-suckles, ripen'd by the sun,
Forbid the sun to enter …

Two good cultivars of this honeysuckle are *L.p.* 'Belgica,' also called Early Dutch, and *L.p.* 'Serotina Florida,' one of the Late Dutch cultivars. 'Belgica' blooms first with purple-red or deep pink flowers and yellowish insides, but 'Serotina Florida' is the more spectacular: it starts flowering in early summer and continues into the fall, with fruit appearing at the same time as a wonderful mass of dark purple flowers that have a variety of creamy white, yellow, and deep red insides.

Honeysuckles grow best in full sun, but they don't mind some shade. I have mine in a variety of soils, none too well prepared, but all are doing fine. They can be pruned lightly after flowering to prevent legginess, but heavy pruning should be done in the spring. There are no serious pests, although they are susceptible to aphids and mites, which are easily controlled with insecticidal soap.

rose

Rosa (ro-zuh)

Where does one begin with roses? Whole gardens and entire lives are devoted to them. And yet, I've only explored a little bit of the landscape of roses. Besides shrub roses like the old-fashioned fragrant pink 'Celsiana' and *Rosa rubrifolia*, with its red foliage, I was satisfied with white *Rosa rugosa* until I started to grow some climbers. It's not that I lack a spirit of adventure; I have had specialty gardens. Once I had a black garden with black poppies, black pinks, black hollyhocks, and black pansies. But that was easy since there's not much choice in such an odd color range. My friends, too, have been inventive—Ellen plotted a Grateful Dead garden with scarlet begonias, sunflowers, sugar magnolias, and American Beauty roses.

Ah! roses—ideal for a vine garden even though they aren't vines; they are woody shrubs with long canes that need at least 4 to 6 hours of sun a day. They're perfect for growing on trellises, especially fan-shaped ones. When the canes are spread out, most roses will sprout more lateral branches.

So where did I begin? I started by looking through books and finding roses that interested me. *Climbing Roses* by Scanniello and Bayard may be the only book you'll need. I first looked for a small rose suitable for a small trellis. While miniature roses have the long canes of climbing roses, they preserve the small flowers and leaves of their miniature bush ancestors. And with the development of climbing miniatures, especially by Ralph Moore in California, there are quite a few to choose from. I chose the pink climber *Rosa* 'Jeanne Lajoie.'

'JEANNE LAJOIE'

'Jeanne Lajoie' has beautiful, medium pink double flowers that fade as they age. The fragrance is light and the well-formed pointed buds usually grow in clusters. The plant has glossy leaves and smooth stems with occasional red prickles. It was introduced in 1975 after being developed by Ed Sima of Seattle, Washington. A member of the Seattle Rose Society, he first developed a popular miniature, the white climber 'Casa Blanca,' which is one of the parents of 'Jeanne Lajoie.' 'Jeanne Lajoie' is very hardy (Zones 5–9), blooms best in cool weather, and is successfully grown far from its first home, in places such as Texas, the Midwest, and the Northeast.

It takes a few years before 'Jeanne Lajoie' will bloom profusely and steadily throughout the summer. In time, it grows well beyond the 6- to 8-foot height listed in catalogues. The canes can reach 12 feet and, because the plant has an upright habit, will naturally arch at half that height. To encourage reblooming, remove the spent flowers after the blooms have faded. Be sure to leave some flowers to set shiny orange hips in the fall.

Other pruning is not necessary, except for the removal of old wood in the winter. 'Jeanne Lajoie' is pretty much disease-resistant.

'SILVER MOON'

After this well-behaved small rose, I splurged on a more extravagant one—the magnificent 'Silver Moon.' I saw a stone wall gloriously festooned with it and thought I should grow it in the one spot I have for a large trellis. If not a stone wall, a pergola or lattice fence is ideal for this rose.

'Silver Moon' was developed by Dr. Van Fleet in 1902 and introduced by the Peter Henderson Company in 1910. From buds with a pale yellow blush at the base come very large, nearly single flowers, which are waxy white with bright yellow stamens. The leaves are a shiny dark green without blemishes. 'Silver Moon' is such a vigorous grower, 8 to 12 feet, that it can be used as a hedge. To grow it on a trellis requires some attention, because it has so many branches. It's especially important to prune out the old wood in the winter so it will not become a knot of unmanageable branches. The prickles are huge and about three per inch, on smooth stems.

My only disappointment with 'Silver Moon' is its short blooming time, which is partially compensated for by large hips in autumn. After a big display of flowers in late spring, an established plant may have occasional blooms later on in the summer.

I generally prefer plants that do not bloom throughout the summer, but there's a limit to my acceptance of brevity. In a stretch of my yellow perennials with *Achillea taygetea* 'Moonshine,' *Coreopsis verticillata* 'Moonbeam,' iris, and daylilies, the focal point is *Trollius ledebourii* 'Golden Queen.' Last year the brief glimpse I had of the globeflower before it was consumed by a gluttonous deer was so frustrating that I decided I needed a yellow replacement, and I thought of roses.

'GOLDEN SHOWERS'

To satisfy my desire for a yellow rose, I planted *Rosa* 'Golden Showers,' developed by Dr. Walter E. Lammerts and introduced in 1956. The following year it was an All-American Rose Selections winner.

'Golden Showers' is an everblooming daffodil-yellow climbing rose with short stems. Although it can reach 15 feet, its usual height is somewhere between 6 and 10 feet. It's the hardiest of yellow climbers, but in the north it tends to be shorter. It takes a few years for long canes to grow from which short laterals will flower. This is what I wanted for my 8-foot trellis.

The long, pointed buds open to 5-inch fragrant, semi-double flowers—an abundance of them throughout the summer and into the fall. The leaves are very dark and glossy. Not much pruning is required, but dead-heading the spent flowers will help stimulate continuous bloom and prevent the development of hips. As the fall approaches let some of the flowers remain for a show of hips.

'Golden Showers' has very few large and curved prickles, making this an easy plant to touch. I am planning to move my 'Ramona' clematis beside it for a nice combination of yellow and pale lavender.

When I need to prune the clematis, there will be no worries about getting scratched by the rose.

There may be greater poetry about roses than this work of Christina Rossetti, but I like her light-hearted praise in "The Rose":

> The lily has an air,
> And the snowdrop a grace,
> And the sweetpea a way,
> And the heartsease a face,—
> Yet there's nothing like the rose
> When she blows.

actinidia

Actinidia kolomikta (ak-ti-NID-ee-uh ko-lo-MIK-tuh)

Nineteenth-century plant explorers discovered the striking *Actinidia kolomikta* in the Far East. In 1856, Carl Maximowicz, a Russian botanist, brought it from the Amur Province of eastern Siberia to St. Petersburg. The English plant sleuth Charles Maries (1851–1902), hunting plants in China and Japan, found it in Sapporo and sent it to England in 1878. Frank Meyer (1875–1918), an American botanist and explorer who loved to travel on foot even in the depths of winter, discovered *Actinidia kolomikta* while working for the United States Department of Agriculture in eastern Asia. Before he disappeared, presumed drowned in the Yangtze, he discovered new varieties of beans, rice, other vegetables, and fruits as well as other ornamentals.

The name *Actinidia* comes from the Greek word *aktis*, meaning "a ray." This alludes to the style, the pillar-like extension from the ovary that is topped by the stigma. The styles of the actinidia radiate like spokes of a wheel. *Kolomikta* is the native name; the range of *A. kolomikta* is northeastern Asia from Japan to central and western China. Like other actinidias, it has edible fruits, and although often called by its botanical name, it is also known as super-hardy kiwifruit, Arctic beauty kiwifruit, Manchurian gooseberry, Amur gooseberry, and Chinese gooseberry.

Actinidia kolomikta adds a dramatic splash of color to the garden. It is a deciduous woody vine grown more often for its foliage than for its fruit. In the spring, the new green leaves of the male plant and—to a lesser degree—of the female, develop bright splotches of white, pink, and occasionally red. This is not subtle—it's almost artificial looking—and it spreads from the tip backwards. But as the leaves age over the summer, the coloration fades and the plant takes on a monochromatic hue. The bright, lime-green leaves are 4 to 6 inches long. They are shaped like elongated hearts, and their texture reminds me of seersucker.

While actinidia can survive in Zones 3–7 in both sun or part shade, it doesn't do well in hot weather. At the same time, it prefers a warm, sheltered position, such as a south-facing wall or fence. Females will not fruit if nipped by a late frost. Actinidia climbs 15 to 20 feet and needs sturdy support for its clockwise-twining growth, but patience is needed because this vine grows slowly, ten feet in ten years, and the coloring takes several years to develop. Colors develop best in full sun.

Actinidia needs a well-drained, well-limed soil that is not too heavily fertilized. If you want the small, smooth-skinned edible yellow fruits, a female should be planted as well as a male. Actinidia has fragrant white flowers with yellow stamens in May or June, followed in the fall by the fruit, which is extremely rich in vitamin C. The fruit is a smaller, smooth-skinned relative of the kiwifruit, *Actinidia deliciosa*. The plant should be pruned to control the size, as well as to remove dead wood. Because it flowers on old wood, you must prune after flowering, but do most of the heavy pruning while the plants are dormant. Lee Reich's book, *Uncommon Fruits Worthy of Attention*, includes detailed information about growing this and the other, larger actinidias.

There are no pests to worry about, except maybe your pets. Cats are attracted to actinidia, especially *A. deliciosa*, and can destroy young plants by clawing and chewing. *A. kolomikta* appears not to have the same draw, in my garden at least. My neighbors' cats spend a lot of time in my garden and have yet to find it of any interest. But the Japanese have called it "Cat's Medicine" for its powerful effects.

clematis

Clematis (KLEM-a-tiss)

My favorite trellis plants are clematis. The name comes from the Greek *klema*, meaning a twig, usually of a vine. Clematis belong to the buttercup family (Ranunculaceae), which includes many familiar plants like *Aquilegia*, *Aconitum*, *Anemone*, *Delphinium*, *Trollius*, and *Thalictrum*. There are so many kinds of clematis to grow that it's worth a trip to a botanical garden or a browse through a book to pick your favorite. Clematis may be the most popular of all vines for the garden because they are tough and elegant, yet manageable. And if you cut them for indoor arrangements with a little of the old wood, they will last for days.

I have found that the spring-blooming, vanilla-scented *Clematis montana*, or anemone clematis, which has small white flowers, and 'Tetrarose,' a rose-pink variety with a spicy scent, are too large for my trellises. But I can't help mentioning them because for many years I stubbornly believed anything could be kept small. Now I've devoted one end of my front porch to 'Tetrarose.' *Montana* means "pertaining to mountains," in this case the Himalayas of central and western China, whence it was first introduced in 1831. Ernest Henry Wilson (1876–1930), a collector so famous for his work in China that he gained the nickname "Chinese Wilson," introduced the variety *C.m.* var. *rubens* in 1900. It blooms after the species and has pink flowers.

Also unsuitable for a trellis is the more common, sweet autumn clematis

C. paniculata. *Paniculata* indicates that the flowers grow in loose, open, branching clusters or panicles. Sometimes it is listed as *Clematis maximowicziana* (max-im-o-wix-ee-a-nuh), named for the Russian botanist Carl Maximowicz (1827–1891). According to E. H. Wilson, the Arnold Arboretum distributed plants of *C. paniculata* grown from seeds received from Russia in 1877. It has a prolific flowering of small, fragrant white flowers, and it's easy to grow. Everyone should plant it, but don't try to restrict it. Mine grows through a lilac, which it smothers with flowers in September.

But there are plenty of choices of clematis for a small 6- to 8-foot trellis. The large-flowered clematis are perfect for Zones 3–9. On my trellises, I've grown only four: the deep violet-purple *Clematis × jackmanii*, the white 'Henryi,' the light lavender-blue 'Ramona,' and a yellow species, *C. tibetana*.

C. × JACKMANII

C. × jackmanii (jak-MAN-ee-i) was the first of the so-called large-flowered varieties. Its purple flowers are 5 to 6 inches across.

The parents of the Jackman clematis are said to be *C. viticella*, sometimes called "Italian clematis" (even though it was introduced to England from Spain in 1569), and *C. lanuginosa*, the woolly-leaved clematis. *C. lanuginosa* was introduced from Ningpo (now Ningbo), China, by the plant explorer Robert Fortune in 1850. Its exceptionally large flowers (usually 8 inches across) made it a logical choice to be selected as a parent of later hybrids.

First raised in England at the Woking nursery of George Jackman and Sons in the 1860s, *C. × jackmanii* was exhibited in Boston in 1866 by Francis Parkman (1823–1893), better known as an historian than a horticulturist. Parkman, author of *The Book of Roses*, was a member of the Massachusetts Horticultural Society and had a garden by Jamaica Pond near the Arnold Arboretum in Boston.

C. 2 *jackmanii* blooms from June, or July in the north, until the frost, in both sun and shade. It will grow 6 to 18 feet high and it blooms on new wood. The flowers have four or five petals—actually sepals, or modified leaves. They are purple with reddish accents. While I think the color is great, I admit to liking garish combinations; for instance, my pink rose 'Jeanne Lajoie' is growing with the orange-red honeysuckle 'Dropmore Scarlet.' Neltje Blanchan must have preferred more harmonious colors, for she wrote the following about C. 2 *jackmanii* in *The American Flower Garden* in 1909:

> Until one's attention is called to it, no one would believe how common is the custom of planting the large-flowered purple Jackman's clematis against red-brick buildings. Yet, when it spreads its royal bloom over them, nothing in the great range of garden possibilities is more excruciatingly awful.

'HENRYI'

Both 'Ramona' and 'Henryi' are *lanuginosa*-type hybrids. When I bought 'Henryi,' I knew it was both popular and old-fashioned. 'Henryi' was raised by Anderson and Henry of Edinburgh and introduced in 1858. No doubt you've seen photographs of it embracing a white porch column. 'Henryi' has pronounced buds in the spring, large creamy white flowers in the summer, and amazing seed heads by fall. Most clematis seed heads last well in dry arrangements, but the 'Henryi' seed heads are especially beautiful. At first, they look like doll wigs with silky spirals. A week later it's not so easy to see this swirling move- ment; instead they look like little dusters with fluffy white clusters of exploded hairs.

'RAMONA'

When I planted 'Ramona'—advertised for its "blue" flowers—I thought I was getting a modern variety, but in fact it has been sold since 1874. In his extensive study of clematis, the British author Ernest Markham wrote that 'Ramona' was an American name given to *Hybrida Sieboldii*, developed by a Dutch nurseryman. Although it is not blue, it is a lighter lavender than C. × *jackmanii*. 'Ramona,' like 'Henryi,' should be cut back to 2 to 4 feet in early spring. Both of these plants bloom on new wood and old. When pruning, the idea is to leave branches that will produce flowers. This means that if some of last year's growth is left, there will be a flowering in June as well as in late summer.

CLEMATIS TEXENSIS

I am looking forward to planting the scarlet—or Texas—clematis, a species with leathery, red bell-shaped flowers that is native to Texas. *Clematis texensis* (teks-EN-sis), formerly known as C. *coccinea* (kok-SIN-ee-uh) and introduced in 1878, has blue-gray foliage and scarlet to rose-pink flowers about 1 inch long in the summer, followed by fluffy seed heads in the fall. It grows about six feet tall, and its range is as far north as Zone 4. If it dies back to the ground—which is common in the north—it will come back the next spring. In either case there will be flowers, because it blooms on new growth. It is a parent of many good hybrids, including the pink-flowered 'Duchess of Albany,' introduced in 1897.

CLEMATIS TIBETANA

In autumn C. *tibetana* (ti-bi-
TAH-nuh) is wonderful.
Individually the small, green-
yellow flowers are not
spectacular, but in the fall—
when there are buds,
flowers, and seed heads all
together—the colors and
textures are beautiful.

C. *tibetana* should be
pruned hard in early spring
because it will grow 10 to
12 feet. It can be difficult to find this
species, but it is similar to C. *orientalis*,
which is more commonly available.

Pruning and Care

It's important to know about pruning clematis or you might cut off the flowering
shoots. While some species flower only on new or old wood, some flower on both.
Plant vines that require pruning at the same time together because it's almost
impossible to disentangle them without breaking the leaf stems. The stems are stiff
and the petiole, or leaf stalk, curls like a tendril and supports the plant as it climbs.
They hold on to their supports as tightly as wire. Large-flowered vines need the
dead wood removed and straggling shoots trimmed as they begin to grow in the
spring. If you don't cut out the old wood, the tangle can be difficult to deal with
because of the stiffness of the criss-crossing stems. Pinching out the new crown
growth will stimulate leafing out of the branches. The very vigorous fall-blooming
vines need severe pruning in the spring when they begin to grow. There are many
good reference books on clematis for those interested in the subtleties of pruning. I
find Christopher Lloyd's *Clematis* especially helpful.

In the wild, clematis vines grow in thickets or on the margins of woods. This means they like shade at their roots, provided by some mulch or a rock, but sun, preferably full sun, for the tops. They do best in rich, well-drained but moist soil with some lime. Because clematis don't like their roots disturbed, plant container-grown specimens. Support is needed for all clematis, and young shoots should be tied. You can give them some protection for early spring by planting them on west or southwest walls.

Clematis can have a variety of problems, including leaf spot, stem rot, wilt, and mildew. Pests that like to eat them include slugs, mice, and rabbits. But if you are watching them closely, as you'll want to be, the problems are minor.

I have not found many poems celebrating the beauty of clematis, but there is plenty of poetry in the common names. Porch vine best describes those growing on trellises, but traveler's joy, devil's thread, virgin's bower, bind-with-love, devil's-hair, gray-beard, smoking-cane, grandfather's whiskers, love-vine, snow-in-harvest, and Father Time conjure up those growing in wilder settings.

porcelain berry

Ampelopsis brevipedunculata (am-pe-LOP-sis bre-vee-pe-dun-kew-LAH-tuh)

Ampelopsis brevipedunculata is in the grape or vine family. Its name comes from the Greek *ampelos* for "vine" and *opsis* for "likeness" because the leaf is similar to that of the grapevine. The leaves are alternate and 5 inches wide with three lobes, and they have a bumpy texture—a puckering from many little veins. *Brevipedunculata* means "with a short flower stalk." It has beautiful berries, from which it gets other names such as turquoise berry, porcelain vine, or blueberry climber. The fruit ranges in color from pale lilac to yellow, bright blue, and turquoise, all at the same time.

I am including porcelain berry because it's easy to grow and beautiful and recommended in many nursery catalogues. However, I have serious reservations since reading an article entitled "Barbarians at Our Gates" in the *American Horticulturalist* news edition. There was a black and white drawing of porcelain berry. Without the beautiful colors of the berries to seduce me, I knew at once I had to rethink including it. Once you see it as a pest, like poison ivy, much of its splendor vanishes. It's a good example of a rampant plant you might think you want if you're new to gardening.

I remember being offered plants that my friends warned me were vigorous, rampant, invasive, and otherwise easy to grow. It only takes a season or two to realize that what you really want is something else, and now you'll have to spend many seasons undoing what you and nature have done. If the common name has "weed" in it—like bishop's weed—question it. Butterfly weed is great, but it pays to check. If someone says that a plant will spread, you might want to say "No, thank you" and ask for a division of something else. Think twice before planting anything if you're not as far north as I am—a wisteria in Key West is not the treasure that it is on Twelfth Street in New York City.

Ampelopsis brevipedunculata comes from northeastern Asia and will grow in Zones 4–8. It climbs by means of twisting, two-pronged tendrils and will not make a dense cover. Prune it while the plant is dormant, but trim new unattached shoots in the summer. This vine will grow in the shade, but the attraction is the berries, which ripen in the fall, and they give the best colors in full sun. I've read only one account that the berries are edible, although they have an insipid taste.

Ampelopsis needs room and support but will do fine with ordinary soil and watering. Sometimes Japanese beetles or caterpillars get into it. It's tolerant of wind; in fact, I warn you, it's a rampant grower. Not only is ampelopsis too big for my trellis, growing 20 feet or more, but it easily spreads beyond control with the help of birds. I pulled it out and am keeping a close watch on one of its cultivars, 'Elegans.'

'ELEGANS'

Ampelopsis brevipedunculata 'Elegans' is said to have been introduced before 1847. It grows more slowly and not quite as far north (Zone 5) as *A. brevipedunculata*. The leaves are smaller and have a nice variegation of spots and stripes that are a combination of pale gray-green, dark green, and a greenish white, with a little pink when young. It is sometimes sold as *Ampelopsis tricolor*. This vine usually grows from 3 to 10 feet, although some sources say it reaches 20 feet. I suspect it depends where you live. Like the species, 'Elegans' flowers on new growth; even if you cut it to the ground in early spring, you will still see the shiny bright blue berries in the fall. It's more temperamental than the species about producing berries—it needs a hot summer and a mild autumn—and birds are quick to eat them. If you pick porcelain vine when the berries start to ripen, it is lovely in flower arrangements.

five-leaf akebia

Akebia quinata (a-KEE-bee-uh kwi-NAY-tuh)

Akebia quinata is another beautiful vine that should be more widely known. It was introduced in about 1845 by Robert Fortune, a Scotsman who explored for plants in China and Japan. His travels, which he described in four books, were so dangerous that he sometimes wore Chinese dress to disguise himself, even wearing a Chinese-style pigtail. Akebia's native home ranges from central China to Korea and Japan. In Japan, the fruits are sometimes eaten, and the shoots are used to make baskets, trays, and hats. *Akebia* comes from the Latinized version of the Japanese name for this vine, "akebi," and *quinata* means "in fives," for the five parts of its leaf.

I grow the vine for its lovely, deep green leaves. It is a twiner, growing clockwise up several of the vertical lengths of the trellis. Every 2 inches or so it has a pale green stem with a leaf comprising five small leaflets arranged like the spread fingers of a hand. Near the top the smaller, younger leaves are more closely spaced and yellower. No insects or diseases bother the vine, giving it a fresh, clean appearance. Plant it where a dense shade is not wanted. If it can be planted so that its beautiful silhouette can be seen or so it will cast patterns on a flat surface, so much the better.

The vine grows quickly from 15 to 40 feet in Zones 4–8. It's good for a trellis as long as you are prepared to prune it. Where the winters are mild (Zone 7) it is evergreen and can grow out of control, but it will recover quickly if cut to the ground in late winter. In any case you can pinch it when young to encourage many stems. In areas where it gets very large, limit it to two or three main trunks. It likes good garden soil, preferably a light one, and will grow in half shade to full sun.

Louise Beebe Wilder's *Colour in My Garden* has a wonderful chapter about familiar plant names. She urges us to recognize and know the Latin names of plants while praising the common names. Her list of plant names includes new names she and her children used, such as "Tricorne Vine" for *Akebia quinata*. Akebia is also called chocolate vine or raisin vine because of the small, very sweet berries produced in the fall. The three-petaled flowers are inconspicuous but fragrant and appear in April or May. It is important to give the plant shelter because if the frost touches the early flowers, there will be no fruit production. Both the male and the female flowers, staminate and pistillate, appear in the same cluster. The staminate are a light purple, fragrant, and smaller (¼ inch across) than the pistillate, which are a dull brownish-purple chocolate color and about 1 inch across. They do not pollinate easily but hand pollinating may help. The fruits are 2 to 4 inches long, purple, and sausage-shaped. Inside are black seeds in a white pulpy flesh once considered worth eating. There are two cultivars of *Akebia quinata*, 'Alba' and 'Rosea.' The first has white flowers and fruits, and the second has flowers more lavender than pink.

Because akebia flowers on old wood, the time to prune lightly is after the flowering. But if you hope for fruit, you need to leave some flowering branches.

trumpet vine
Campsis radicans (KAMP-sis RAD-i-kanz)

The trumpet vine, or trumpet-creeper, has gained the name *Campsis* from the Greek word *kampe*, meaning "something bent." This refers to the stamens of the trumpet vine, which are curved. *Radicans* is Latin for "with rooting stems," which describes its growth habit and suggests the ease with which it can be rooted from cuttings. *C. radicans* is a native of the southeast United States and is widespread throughout New England. While it was first introduced into Europe commercially by 1640, even the less-known yellow cultivar 'Flava' has been around since 1842.

The tubular flowers are 4 to 6 inches long and grow in clusters, but only on the part of the plant exposed to the sun. The plant must be well established before it blooms at all. The flowers, and seed pods at the end of the summer, are big and chunky. There's nothing delicate about them, except the hummingbirds that like to visit, a phenomenon noted by Mark Catesby (1679–1749) in the early 1700s. On one of his two trips to the New World, Catesby described how the trumpet vine's flower is adapted to the ruby-throated hummingbird: the bright red corollas attract them, while the fleshy insides protect the flower from the long beak by which they're pollinated. In Europe the plant is called the hummingbird vine. Catesby introduced to Britain a tree in the same family, the *Catalpa bignoides*. I mention this because we have two catalpas supporting a hammock. Despite some of the catalpa's messy habits, I find it spectacular and like to remember its relationship to the trumpet vine.

Trumpet vines will grow in a tough spot, thriving in full sun and rich soil. The leaves are compound with toothed leaflets. But a plant with a height of 30 feet is not my idea of a plant for a trellis, even if it attracts hummingbirds. It tends to make so much new growth that the base will become bare unless it's pinched back regularly.

Cut back the flowering shoots as the flowers are shed in late summer. When pruning seriously, save only a few main stalks and shorten the laterals on these. In the winter spade out the root suckers at the base of the plant, or grow the plant in confined beds to prevent its spread by root suckers. The main stem will cling to a wall with aerial rootlets. Some say the tendrils cling so tightly that they can damage roofs and masonry.

Although native to Japan, *Campsis grandiflora* (gran-di-FLO-ra) is known as the Chinese trumpet-creeper. It was found by Engelbert Kaempfer (1652–1728) in Japan in 1691, although not introduced until much later. Kaempfer is well known to gardeners; his name was given to many plants including Japanese iris, *Iris kaempferi*. This vine is hardy in Zones 7–9, which include the South, the Southeast north to Virginia, and the West Coast. Because it doesn't grow as tall as *C. radicans* and the flowers are a bright red-orange and a little larger, it is considered one of the best of the trumpet vines. The salmon red variety I grow is *Campsis × tagliabuana* (tag-lee-a-BWA-na) 'Madame Galen.' It was developed from a cross of *C. grandiflora* and *C. radicans* and is named for the Tagliabue brothers, Italian nurserymen who made the cross. It was introduced into the trade in 1889 and is hardy in Zones 4–9.

I haven't seen a dwarf trumpet vine, but in one of my older gardening books there's a mention of one, *Tecoma radicans* var. *speciosa*. *Campsis* was previously known as *Tecoma*, from the Mexican name of the species, *Tecomaxochitl*.

Michael Dirr, whose *Manual of Woody Landscape Plants* is a wonderful source of information, writes about the trumpet vine: "If you cannot grow this, give up gardening; grows in any soil and also prospers in sidewalk cracks. . . ." Alice Lounsberry wrote of it in her 1901 book *Southern Wild Flowers and Trees*:

> . . . the southern natives . . . call it devil's shoestrings because its interlaced growth hinders their progress, or even more contemptuously, 'cowitch,' in reference to the belief that when cows eat of it the effect in their milk is harmful. Quite generally they regard it as poisonous. In fact they approach it with much more caution than they do poison ivy.

Trumpet vines can be grown on lattices, carefully threaded through the slats, but not on trellises. They're simply too big. My *Campsis × tagliabuana* 'Madame Galen' grew too big for a trellis its first year in the garden. It grew more than 20 feet, and many branches spread out and rooted between my perennials. I think it's best to grow it on a pergola or pillar.

firethorn

Pyracantha coccinea (pye-ruh-KAN-thuh kok-SIN-ee-uh) **'Mohave'**

Like the climbing rose, the evergreen firethorn is a member of the rose family that, although not a vine, can be trained to grow on a trellis. It has stiff and thorny branches that can be used as a hedge or espaliered into a decorative pattern on a trellis or wall. Sometimes firethorns are even sold ready-shaped into a dense design on a small trellis. *Pyracantha* comes from the Greek words for "fire," *pur*, and "thorn," *akantha*. The thorns make training a delicate matter because the prickly branches must be fixed in place with some sort of tie. *Coccinea* comes from the Latin *coccineus* for "scarlet-colored."

    P. c. 'Mohave' has attractive small white flowers in the spring, followed by crimson berries in the fall and winter—a beautiful addition to the evergreen plant, which is covered with small, shiny, dark green leaves. This particular variety was developed with features that discourage birds from eating the berries, to provide a colorful display in fall and winter. The fruit will develop best if firethorns are grown in full sun. There are many varieties, and some demand a little less sun.

    'Mohave' grows to 10 feet and most varieties grow well in Zones 6–9, but the range is broadened by careful choosing for your zone and local microclimate. Once established, they shouldn't be moved. They are somewhat drought-tolerant and need a well-drained soil. In addition, they are good for city plantings because they are unaffected by pollution.

    Firethorns need to be protected from pests. Like apples and pears they belong to the rose family and serve as hosts to the apple scab fungus and other diseases of rosaceous fruits. Don't grow firethorns if you live near an orchard or have prize collections of pear or crabapple trees. Lime sulphur sprayed on the plant before the buds open helps to prevent scab. Fireblight, a bacterial disease that blackens the stems and leaves so that the plant looks burned, is difficult to control and a terrible problem where summers are hot and humid. 'Mohave' is quite resistant to both scab and fireblight. Other potential problems are scale, aphids, leaf blight, lace bugs, and spider mites.

Firethorns look wonderful in containers and can be pruned anytime. For espaliering, it's best to prune them after flowering. When they are young, prune to develop a well-branched bush. Cut back the new growth as you wish because flowers form on the older wood. Firethorns can be trained to formal shapes like a fan. With climbing roses, or with other firethorns with differently colored berries, many beautiful combinations can be discovered.

wintercreeper

Euonymus fortunei var. radicans (yew-ON-i-mus for-TU-nee-i RAD-ik-ans) **'Variegatus'**

I used to find variegated leaves a bit fussy and distracting in the garden, but then I grew *Euonymus fortunei* var. *radicans* 'Variegatus.' The leaves of this variety of wintercreeper are small and emphatically marked green and white. In my garden it grows as a spreading shrub, or ground cover, and also against a white trellis where I especially love its effect with the painted white wood.

The name *Euonymus* comes from the Greek name for the spindle-tree, which they called "of good name," *fortunei* refers to the plant explorer Robert Fortune (1812–1880), and *radicans* means "with rooting stems." Robert Fortune spent almost twenty years collecting plants in China and Japan for the Horticultural Society of London. He introduced bleeding-heart, Japanese anemone, balloon flower, and forsythia, to name just a few of his contributions. *Euonymus fortunei* made its first appearance in 1907, and many cultivars have been developed since then. Because there are so many variations, expect to find overlap and confusion when buying plants.

Wintercreeper is often recommended for planting around a front door because it can be clipped flat and the branches and leaves make beautiful patterns. Because it's hardy in Zones 5–10, it is one of the few reliable evergreen vines for the north. Plant it in a shady position or on a north wall, however, so that the winter sun won't burn the leaves. If wintercreeper is killed by cold weather it will die back to the ground.

It takes ten years for wintercreeper to reach 10 to 12 feet. As it climbs on either wood or brick, it will make small rootlike holdfasts on the stem facing away from the light. (It is easy to propagate with stem cuttings or layering.) There are many forms of wintercreeper to choose from besides 'Variegatus.' Leaves of other cultivars may be solid green or have pink or yellow coloring and different patterns of stripes or markings around the edges. The flowers in spring are a greenish white and inconspicuous, and the berries are not very noticeable either: pale pink capsules open in September to reveal orange pulp covering the seeds.

Wintercreeper likes part shade and moist but well-drained soil. Any dead, broken, or diseased branches should be pruned in early spring. Euonymus scale can be a problem. Scale insects look like small bumps on the foliage and stems, most often on the undersides of the leaves. If these symptoms appear, spray the plant with dormant oil in the winter or early spring; use horticultural oil (also called superior oil or summer oil) in the summer.

Euonymus grows well with clematis. The contrasting leaf sizes and colors look lovely, and the wintercreeper provides shade for the clematis roots.

everlasting pea

Lathyrus latifolius (LA-thi-rus la-ti-FOH-lee-us)

The everlasting pea, *Lathyrus latifolius*, is a quick-growing, sometimes rampant perennial vine. It's often seen in a mound and is usually 4 to 10 feet tall. *Lathyrus* is from the Greek *lathuros*, a kind of pea, and *latifolius* is Latin for "broad-leaved." The winged stems are supported by tendrils. But what I really like is the angular way in which the plant grows—almost zigzagging up the support. These peas are recommended for seaside gardens and the most inhospitable places. In good soil it can become a pest.

With average garden soil and moisture, the perennial pea will flower all summer, but only if nights are cool. In either full sun or light shade, it is beautiful. The long branches have foot-long stems with five to seven flowers. I have a rose-pink plant, but there are white cultivars, such as 'White Pearl,' and seeds are sold in mixes of pinks and whites. These flowers last well in arrangements and look very nice in a vase with clematis. Everlasting peas are old favorites for cottage gardens. They're wonderful growing through shrubs or mounding and hiding perennials that have finished blooming.

sweet pea

Lathyrus odoratus (LA-thi-rus oh-do-RAY-tus)

Lathyrus odoratus is what we think of when extolling the virtues of the sweetness of peas, as Keats did in his untitled poem:

> *Here are sweet peas, on tip-toe for a flight:*
> *With wings of gentle flush o'er delicate white,*
> *And taper fingers catching at all things,*
> *To bind them all about with tiny wings.*

The perennial pea is a weed compared to the annual *Lathyrus odoratus*, a native of south Sicily. It was first introduced to England in 1699. Franciscus Cupani, an Italian monk, published a description of it in *Hortus Catholicus* in 1697 and sent seeds to England. The development of sweet peas really began in about 1870 thanks largely to Henry Eckford (1823–1905), who devoted the last third of his life to them. By 1900 there were so many varieties of sweet peas that a Crystal Palace exhibit in London featured 264 varieties. From one of Eckford's plain, or smooth varieties, 'Prima Donna,' came a frilled form grown and introduced by Silas Cole, an English gardener. 'Countess Spencer,' first exhibited in 1910, is the variety from which practically all modern sweet peas have been developed.

I am a newcomer to these truly sweet-smelling peas because I was worried that they would be too demanding. In fact, with a little effort—as well as your best soil and best spot—they will bloom.

The annual sweet peas grow to about 6 feet, with some differences in height and fragrance depending on the variety. They climb by their tendrils and need delicate trellises, strings, or wires to hold on to. The fragrant 2-inch flowers are borne one to four on a stem; improved types are heat-tolerant and bloom all summer. A catalogue from the 1700s is reported to have described the fragrance as "somewhat like Honey and a little tending to the Orange-flower Smell."

If sweet pea flowers are not cut, they will stop blooming and go to seed. As one who does not often take advantage of the flowers in her garden by bringing them indoors, I must remind myself of this. Enjoy them! Cut them! Bring them indoors! Sweet peas should flower from July to October if planted in deeply trenched, heavy soil. If you're better organized than I am, make three sowings to ensure a succession of bloom. Try interplanting them with nasturtiums: when the sweet peas are finished blooming, the nasturtiums will continue until frost. Sweet peas prefer a cool climate and even moisture.

Generally, sweet peas are best grown in the cool climates of Zones 5 and below. In the New York area, prepare a trench with 3 inches of deeply dug soil enriched with a good mixture of manure. The surface of the trench should be 5 inches below the ground. Sow the seed in mid-March and cover it with 2 inches of good soil. As the seedlings grow, continue to add soil, keeping only the tip of new growth above ground. The roots will be deep and there will be no problems with surface droughts. Protect the seedlings from frost with a layer of newspaper or other mulch. As the plants grow, more soil can be built up to protect them from wind. When they are 4 inches high, they should be pinched back so that side shoots will develop. Give them plenty of water. In Zones 8–10, the seeds can be planted in late summer or early fall for early spring blooms.

Watch for aphids, red spider, and mildew. It's harder to see mice moving or removing the sown seeds or sparrows stealing seedlings when building their nests.

morning glory

Ipomoea (ip-o-MEE-uh)

The *Ipomoea* species offer many wonderful vines for the trellis, and the differences between them are so dramatic you will probably want to plant two or three. The name comes from the Greek *ips*, meaning "wood-worm," and *homoios* meaning "like or resembling." You can count on all of the following *Ipomoea* vines to twine clockwise and to have alternate leaves and funnel-shaped, five-lobed flowers. But the wealth of variation in form and color of both leaves and flowers offers much to choose from. There are heart-shaped leaves as well as finely cut ones, some leaves are variegated and others are not, and the flowers can be narrow and trumpetlike or broad and flat like plates.

In my garden I've been dismayed by a vigorously self-sowing pink variety. Beware of unwanted seedlings (and other unwanted guests). These adaptable plants will persist once they are well established.

The morning glory is one of the most familiar of all flowers, climbing or not. Referring to the wild bindweed, Thoreau wrote about it in his *Journal* from 1852: "It always refreshes me to see it . . . I associate it with the holiest morning hours." Because of their rapid growth and handsome flowers they're often used on porches. As long ago as the eighteenth century, the botanist and plant collector William Bartram (1739–1823), son of John Bartram,

"Father of American Botany," shaded his arbors near Philadelphia with morning glories and gourds. He illustrated many of his findings, including the morning glory, in *Travels through North and South Carolina, Georgia, East and West Florida*, published in 1791.

IPOMOEA TRICOLOR 'HEAVENLY BLUE'

The lovely blue of 'Heavenly Blue' is seen growing 10 to 15 feet or more on fences and up lampposts and mailboxes in the city and country. It is one of many cultivars developed from the tender perennial *Ipomoea tricolor* (three-colored), which some sources cite as dwarf morning glory. It was first described in 1621 by John Goodyer, who assisted Johnson in his edition of Gerard's *Herball*, and already he saw "a most excellent fair skie-coloured blew, so pleasant to behold, that often it amazeth the spectator."

The history of 'Heavenly Blue' is told by Lyman N. White, who worked for Ferry-Morse Seeds, in his book *Heirlooms and Genetics*. The seed was discovered by an amateur seed saver named Clarke in the 1920s. A Dutchman named Nanne Sluis bought Clarke's seed in Colorado and, after growing it in southern France, he had enough seed to sell to American companies. Ferry-Morse had been growing a selection also called 'Heavenly Blue' that didn't bloom in Michigan because of the short growing season there. (This 'Heavenly Blue' may have been already well known by 1910 in California, where the season is longer.) The new seeds from Sluis, originally called 'Clarke's Early Flowering Sky Blue,' were such a success that they became the only strain sold and acquired the name 'Heavenly Blue.'

IPOMOEA PURPUREA 'SCARLET STAR'

Other good cultivars have also been developed from *I. purpurea* (pur-POOR-ree-a, meaning "purple"), probably the parent of most of the common morning glories. *I. purpurea* is a hardy annual. You should be forewarned that it is often hard to know exactly what's what, since books and mail order catalogues often don't cite parentage or they identify it incompletely. In any event, there are many colors to choose from, including white, pink, red, violet and blue. Many morning glories feature flowers with white edges, stars, or stippling; others have leaves that are variegated, heart-shaped or lobed. I planted a pretty red-and-white *Ipomoea purpurea* 'Scarlet Star' (sometimes identified as *I. nil* or *I. hederacea*), that grew to only 4 feet but continued to bloom well into the afternoon.

I. purpurea grows rapidly to 10 to 15 feet with twining stems that branch from the base. It grows well in sun and in rich, light, well-drained soil, but if the soil is too rich it will produce an abundance of leaves instead of flowers. Morning glories will not flourish in extreme heat, but they can withstand a drought. Soak the seeds overnight in water before planting, or notch them with a file and sow outdoors when the ground is warm. Thin them to 18 inches apart or you'll have too many plants with too much weight. Support should not have a circumference greater than 5 inches. The planting season in the New York area is mid-April for flowers at the end of July. If sown indoors in mid-March, and transplanted outside at the beginning of May, morning glories will flower at the end of June.

The properties of certain morning glories make some people think twice about having them in the garden. The seeds of *I. violacea* have alkaloids similar to LSD; the Zapotec Indians in Mexico use them for ceremonies and cures. You should know, too, that *I. violacea* is often confused with *I. tricolor*. As far as I'm concerned, if the garden is to be my place of purity, it must also be a place of peace and safety. So I remind myself that the seeds are okay—as long as nobody eats them. Just as most gardeners find a place for foxgloves and other plants that are dangerous only if we have them for dinner, I've decided morning glories are fine. (People with small children might make a different decision.) I can eat scarlet runner beans or nasturtiums if I need to snack off the vines in my garden. Of greater concern to me is the speed and power of a growing morning glory—like the one growing through my front porch floor. But by staying close to the house, the morning glories may not be devoured by deer. Their primary pest is usually aphids.

JAPANESE MORNING GLORY

There are several names associated with the Japanese morning glory. You will find them listed as Imperial Japanese morning glory or white-edge morning glory, and offered from various sources under *Ipomoea nil*, *I. imperialis*, and *I. hederacea*. *Nil* is Sanskrit for "indigo," the color of the flowers from the tropics. *I. hederacea* (hed-er-AY-see-uh), meaning "like *Hedera*, or ivy," sometimes known as ivy-leaved morning glory, is often confused with *I. nil*, but it is distinguished by the shape of its sepals, which are contracted into linear, recurved, or spreading tips. *Pharbitis nil* and *P. n. Choisy* are former names of *I. nil* that are still occasionally in use.

Despite its name, the Japanese morning glory is most often said to be a tropical American species that was improved in Japan. Curiously, the history of the Japanese morning glory told by the Japanese is diametrically opposed to the western version. They believe that the seeds were brought from southeast Asia to Japan for medicinal use more than a thousand years ago. Another explanation is that Chinese species were brought to Japan with Buddhism and first planted in temple gardens.

In the early 1800s there was a craze in Japan for improved types of morning glories with names like "emperor" and "imperial." They had large flowers, single or double, fringed or ruffled, and of various contrasting colors. A single seed that might have cost fifty cents in 1830 was valued at eighteen dollars in an account from 1911. How much would that be today? Adjusted for inflation, the price was as extravagant as the prices paid in the tulip craze of the seventeenth century.

Japanese morning glories have been developed for pot culture so they are smaller than other types, and they have more branching stems. Today there is a market for their display at the Kishibojin Temple in Tokyo every year in early July. Some of the new hybrids are very unlike the species—there are even varieties that look like clumps of grass with colored tips. Florence DuCane, writing about Japanese gardens and morning glories in 1908, said that they are "best seen at four o'clock in the morning of a scorching July or August day . . . the buds will just be opening, the faded flowers of yesterday will have fallen, and all will be fresh and make you forget the heat of the day that is dawning."

Despite the huge variety of morning glories available in Japan, relatively few are available in the United States. 'Scarlett O'Hara' is one of the most popular cultivars of *I. nil*. Another attractive choice is *I. imperialis* 'Chocolate,' which has lovely, light creamy brown flowers. The one shown here might be 'Light of Sagami,' but the wood-chuck wreaked such havoc that I'm not sure.

moonflower
Ipomoea alba

Another prized *Ipomoea* species is the moonflower, moon vine, or evening glory. It is similar to a morning glory but in giant form. The white flowers are about 6 to 8 inches in diameter and open in the evening, giving off a wonderful and intense fragrance.
Moon vine used to be called *Calonyction aculeatum* (kal-oh-NIK-tee-on ak-YEW-lee-ah-tum)—good to know if you enjoy reading old garden books. This name is still sometimes used in nursery catalogues, where moonflower is always recommended. *Calonyction* is from the Greek *kalos*, for "beautiful," and *nux*, for "night," because

of its nighttime blooming. *Aculeatum* is Latin for "with prickles." Other names include *Ipomoea grandiflora, I. noctiphiton, I. noctiflora,* and *I. bona-nox,* but the correct name for moonflower is simply *Ipomoea alba.* Do not confuse this species with the white cultivar of common morning glory, *I. purpurea* 'Alba.'

Moonflower is a tropical perennial in Zones 9 to 10, but it is easily grown as an annual in the north. In addition, the vine will climb twice as far as the common morning glory, often 10 to 30 feet. The 8-inch leaves are heart-shaped, and the stem is very firm and a little fleshy, with the texture of a rubber hose. In south Florida, moonflower remains evergreen and blooms all year. It tends to be weedy there, but when well controlled, it is a spectacular addition to the garden.

I grow several moonflowers every year, some on trellises and others with lilacs. One from Japan has a lovely pink eye. Unfortunately the deer are as devoted to them as I am—by September the one closest to the woods was missing most of its leaves. Away from the deer, they make an excellent screen. As the flowers develop they become very sculptural, with long twisted buds opening into flat, saucerlike plates. The broad corolla has a long slender tube. Moonflowers bloom in the evening but may stay well into the next morning if it's overcast. To encourage a longer blooming and have the best of all possible worlds, plant them on both east and west walls. They will open earlier in the evening if they are on an east wall, but they will last longer the next morning if they are on the west. They can be propagated with cuttings or seeds. The developing seed head is also decorative, and the harvested seeds are large. Before planting, you should cut or file the seeds or let them soak in water for a day. Sow them 2 inches deep outdoors in May, or indoors between January and March.

With patience, you can actually watch the flowers open in the evening. Children aren't the only ones delighted by the slow motion of the opening buds. Allen Lacy says they can open in under a minute if the evening is warm, but I have yet to see it.

Many poems have been written on moonflowers including one by the ailing Japanese poet, Masa-oka Shiki (1866–1902):

> I think of making a trellis
> > For moonflowers to climb—
> But maybe my life can hardly last
> > Till autumn time.

cypress vine

Ipomoea quamoclit (KWAH-moh-clit)

Cypress vine is a tropical American vine that used to be known as *Quamoclit pennata* and *Q. vulgaris*. *Quamoclit* comes from the Mexican name for this vine that we call cypress vine, star glory, cupid flowers, or Indian pink; *pennata* (pen-NAY-tuh) means "feathered" and refers to the feathery foliage. Peter Henderson, the American plantsman, reported in his 1881 book *Henderson's Handbook of Plants* a Greek derivation for *quamoclit: kuamos* means "kidney bean," and *klitos* means "dwarf." A floral dictionary from around 1876, *The Floral Kingdom*, calls *quamoclit* an "aboriginal Mexican name" however, and assigns to the cypress vine the sentiment of "attachment."

Cypress vine appears in old catalogues and is still available, but since it is widely naturalized in the south it is not often sold commercially. The McElwain Brothers from Southfield, Massachusetts, recommended it in their 1865 catalogue:

"The fine foliage and graceful form of these plants render them an indispensable ornament for green-house or conservatory. . . ." Thomas Jefferson grew it at Monticello in 1790. In 1901, the garden writer Alice Lounsberry reported, "Outside of Jacksonville [Florida], at an ostrich farm, I saw it blooming in great patches on the ground apparently that the gawky birds, with their love of colour, might have the simple pleasure of trampling it down."

Cypress vine is a vigorous threadlike vine with dark green, feathery, finely divided leaves. In sun or part shade, it grows 10 to 20 feet, producing small white, orange, or scarlet flowers. The tubular flowers are 1 to 1½ inches long and show a perfect star at the apex, but they are completely closed in full sun. They're usually in pairs and very pretty as they bloom from July to October.

As with other ipomoeas, cypress vines can be planted outdoors in May or indoors in March or April. They need good drainage but even moisture. Soak or score the seeds and plant them 12 inches apart, and no more than ½ inch deep. They are best grown on a fine network of support such as wire or string. By planting different colors, you can achieve interesting effects. The daintiness of the delicate and fernlike leaves gives an impression of density when in fact there is not enough foliage to provide shade. Cypress vine is free from insects and diseases.

cardinal climber

Ipomoea × multifida (mul-ti-FID-uh)

The cardinal climber, or cardinal vine is a cross between the cypress vine, *Ipomoea quamoclit*, and *I. coccinea* (kok-SIN-ee-a). It is similar to the feathery cypress vine but has broader leaves. This hybrid was raised by Logan Sloter of Ohio and was previously known as *I. × sloteri* (SLOH-ter-rye), also seen as *Quamoclit × sloteri*. It has other common names as well: hearts-and-loving vine, hearts-and-honey, and a variety with yellow throats called hearts-and-flowers.

One of the cardinal climber's parents, *Ipomoea coccinea,* formerly *Quamoclit coccinea* (*coccineus* is the Latin word for "scarlet-colored"), is the star ipomoea, also known as the wild cypress vine, star or red morning glory, or scarlet star glory. Its tubular, light scarlet or yellowish flowers are 1 to 2 inches long. Although similar to those of the cardinal climber, the leaves of star ipomoea have a distinctive pointed heart shape. Star ipomoea can be found growing wild in the southeastern United States.

The cardinal climber grows to about 10 feet. It has 2-inch flowers slightly larger than those of the cypress vine. The cultivation requirements are the same as for the others in this family. It likes full sun but can tolerate some shade. Germination requires 5 to 10 days. The seeds have a tough coat and should be either notched or soaked in lukewarm water for no more than eight hours prior to planting.

I am drawn to the cardinal climber, as are hummingbirds and butterflies.

sweet potato vine

Ipomoea batatas (ba-TAH-tas) 'Blackie'

Sweet potatoes are grown for their edible tubers, but ornamental sweet potatoes are not. They were first developed for their beautiful foliage in 1959 and 1960 at the University of California, and there are now numerous varieties with leaves of many shapes, textures, and colors.

I have grown *Ipomoea batatas* 'Blackie' strictly for its black foliage. Like most of the other ipomoeas, it comes from the tropics and is unable to withstand a frost. The new leaves are green and deeply lobed but very quickly become deep purple. At times the plant has a purple glow, but in other lights it looks like black velvet. The undersides remain a purplish red.

'Blackie' is a climber, but it needs to be strapped to the trellis, where it will grow 6 to 10 feet in full sun. Left in the garden it makes a luxurious dark spreading plant that roots as it goes along. If cut for a flower arrangement, 'Blackie' will last well while rooting in the water. Best of all may be to grow it in a hanging basket and let it cascade down the sides.

spanish flag
Ipomoea lobata (lo-BAH-tuh)

Popularly known as Spanish flag, flag-of-Spain, Mexican morning glory, crimson star glory, exotic love, or dancing ladies, *Ipomoea lobata* is one of the less commonly grown ipomoeas. Like the names of other members of this genus, its name has been changed. It is most often seen as *Mina lobata*—*Mina* after Joseph Mina of Mexico and *lobata* for the deeply lobed leaves. Earlier names also include *Quamoclit lobata* and *Ipomoea versicolor*. *Versicolor* means "variously colored." Spanish flag has been mentioned in garden publications in the United States since at least 1886.

Spanish flag is another easy-to-grow tropical perennial from Mexico, and Central and South America. In Zones 8–10 it's a perennial, but in the north we grow it as an annual. Its twining purplish stems can grow 15 to 20 feet, but in my garden it was half that height. Up to twelve 1-inch bag-shaped flowers grow on each of the long dainty flower spikes, which are forked at the base. They start off with orange-red buds opening to crimson flowers that gradually fade to orange, lemon yellow, and finally to a creamy white. All of the gradations appearing together produce a bicolor effect of yellow and red. The flower tubes never quite open in the north, unless the first frost comes late, but they are prettiest before they open anyway. If they open, they do so from the base to the apex. In my garden, Spanish flag is a great vine for late season bloom.

Before planting, the seeds should be soaked in cold water overnight. They are small, so it is difficult to notch or file them although you can rub them between two pieces of sandpaper. Germination takes 7 to 10 days. Start them indoors in March and plant them outdoors in May when the ground is warm, or sow the seed directly outside after all danger of frost is past.

nasturtium

Tropaeolum majus (tro-PEE-ol-um MAY-jus)

The familiar nasturtium, or Indian cress, is an annual from South America. *Tropaeolum majus* has intensely colored flowers and beautiful round leaves.

Tropaeolum was named by Carolus Linnaeus (1707–1778), the Swedish botanist and explorer who created the binomial system for naming plants that we use today. The name comes from the Greek *tropaion*, a "trophy or monument to an enemy's defeat." Growing on a pillar, the plant apparently looked like a classical trophy: a tree trunk with the round shields of a defeated enemy and their golden helmets streaked with blood. In 1762 Linnaeus's daughter Elizabeth Christina observed: "the flowers of the Nasturtium emit spontaneously, at certain intervals, sparks like electric ones, visible only in the evening." Goethe too observed this, but modern science has not.

According to Peter Henderson, *Tropaeolum* species were introduced in 1596, and many varieties have appeared since 1830. Jean de La Quintinye (1626–1688) described the seeds of nasturtiums thus: "the figure of the *Seed* is a little pyramidal divided by Ribs, having all its superficies engraven and wrought all over, being of a gray colour, inclining to a light Cinnamon." His work, *The compleat gard'ner,* was translated from the French by John Evelyn, author of *Kalendarium Hortense, The Gard'ner's almanac* (1664). Evelyn also tells how to pickle nasturtium seeds.

Nasturtiums are mentioned by the Spanish botanist and physician Nicholas Monardes (1493–1588), for whom *Monarda,* a genus of aromatic herbs of the mint family was named, in his 1569 book on New World plants (English translation from 1577). By 1597 the plants had been introduced to England.

Young nasturtiums are good in salads. The flowers are edible as well as decorative, and the leaves have a delicious peppery taste. They are rich in vitamin C and contain a tasty mustard oil similar to that of watercress *Nasturtium officinale,* whence the common names Indian cress and nasturtium. *Nasturtium* is the Latin name for a kind of cress, from *nasus* for "nose" and *tortus* for "twisting," or together, "nose-turning," for its pungent smell. Some people pick the seed pods to eat fresh, but when tiny and green (just after the flower has withered), the soft green fruits can be pickled as a substitute for capers, as the British did during the Second World War when capers were unavailable. They are good made into a sauce and served with steamed vegetables.

You can also make nasturtium flowers and leaves into nice hors d'oeuvres. Pick a bunch of nasturtium flowers that are in good condition and all about the same size. Remove the pistils and fill the interiors with chopped smoked salmon mixed with capers, chopped parsley, and a small amount of Sauce Chantilly (homemade mayonnaise lightened with whipped cream). Fold the petals over the filling, place in a serving dish, and sprinkle with oil, vinegar, salt, and pepper before serving.

Or, pick a bunch of nasturtium leaves—also about the same size. Chop together hard-cooked egg yolks, chervil, tarragon, anchovies, and capers. Season to taste with salt and pepper. Mix with bread crumbs moistened with milk. Place a teaspoonful of this filling in the center of each leaf, roll up the leaf to enclose the filling, and tie it. Simmer for 5 minutes in a court-bouillon made of white wine seasoned with thyme and a bay leaf. Drain the stuffed leaves, place them in a serving dish, and serve with Sauce Rémoulade or Sauce Chantilly. Decorate the dish with nasturtium flowers.

Gardeners often plant nasturtiums in the vegetable garden because of their distinctive aroma, which is rumored to keep aphids, white flies, and cucumber beetles away. Slugs and snails, on the other hand, love to eat their leaves. Nasturtiums are said to enhance the flavor of ginger and radishes by giving them a good hot taste when grown nearby.

For best flowering, nasturtiums need more than four hours of sun, cool evenings, and even moisture. By late August, if not before, they are ablaze with colors. Schuyler Mathews, a turn-of-the-century author of books about flowers, describes the nasturtium:

> What a glory of color it brings us!—golden yellow, palest straw color, the same tint with ruby eyes, rich maroon, burning scarlet, intense red, delicate salmon, russet-orange, bright orange, aesthetic old gold, and gray-purple in silky sheen, peach-blow pink, streaky bronze and gold, ruby-eyed gold, and a host of variations which I never could adequately describe in twenty pages.

What more can I say? They are also wonderful cut flowers.

Nasturtiums climb by twisting the leaf petioles around the support of the trellis. The stems are thick and succulent and should be assisted up the support before they become a fragile tangle difficult to unravel without breaking. They can grow

8 to 12 feet, but some of the many varieties are dwarf—only inches high. Mine are often somewhere in between, growing no higher than 6 feet.

Like all *Tropaeolum* species, nasturtiums can be propagated by cuttings and seeds. Seeds started indoors in mid-March will flower in early June. If sown outdoors they'll flower in the middle of July. Think carefully about where you want them to grow because they don't transplant well.

The nasturtium is a good flower for the forgetful gardener. It's easy to grow, not only because it germinates easily, but because it likes poor soil and dry weather. It will keep on blooming until it's killed by the frost.

canary bird vine
Tropaeolum peregrinum (per-eg-GRYE-num)

One of the best yellow annual climbers is the canary bird vine, also known as canary vine, canary creeper, or canary bird flower, *Tropaeolum peregrinum*. *Peregrinum* means "foreign" or "strange." In England in the nineteenth century it was called American creeper. It is native to the Andes of Peru and Ecuador and, according to Peter Henderson, was first introduced in 1596. Although less well known than the nasturtium today, it deserves to be planted just as frequently. Canary bird vine is a tender annual growing 8 to 10 feet with beautiful, small, five-lobed leaves, all a uniform lettuce green in color. It flowers from the beginning of July until the frost. A small light yellow flower grows from each leaf axil. This is the fanciful canary with fringed upper petals and green spurs. Occasionally, you might run into an obsolete name, *T. canariense* (ka-nar-e-EN-se).

Like the nasturtium, it is easy to grow and climbs by its leaf petioles. Because it doesn't transplant well it should be started in peat pots for an early planting. The canary bird vine needs more moisture and less sun than the nasturtium; otherwise their cultivation is the same. Because it prefers cool weather and was recommended by a friend in Alaska, I planted it on the north side of the house. By mid-September it was 15 feet high and covered with blooms.

flame flower

Tropaeolum speciosum (spek-ee-OH-sum)

A native of southern Chile, *Tropaeolum speciosum* is said to stop tourists in their tracks. Not surprisingly, this is reflected in the name *speciosum*, which is Latin for "showy." The common name is even more descriptive: flame flower or creeper, flame nasturtium, or Scottish flame thrower.

The flowers bloom in late summer. They have five flat bright vermillion petals with 1-inch long spurs. Flame flower is a perennial in Zones 7–10 and climbs 6 to 10 feet, showing six-lobed light green leaves that look like hands. Since germination can take more than a year, it's easier to buy a plant.

Flame flower likes a shady location in the garden with cool, moist, peaty soil. There will probably be little growth the first season, but with lots of water, it should reach 6 feet in the second season. If you live in the Pacific Northwest, your flame flower will be right at home; it needs cool moist soil and heavy dews in the late summer when it blooms. The red flowers are followed by bright blue fruits. Grown with climbing hydrangeas or on the shady side of a dark conifer, it's quite beautiful.

love-in-a-puff

Cardiospermum halicacabum (kar-dee-oh-SPER-mum hal-ik-KAK-ab-um)

Love-in-a-puff, *Cardiospermum halicacabum*, equally well named balloon-vine, heart-seed, heart-pea, heart vine, or winter cherry, gets its name from the Greek *kardia*, meaning "heart," and *spermum*, meaning "seed." *Halicacabum* is from the Greek word for winter cherry. Picked when fresh, the seeds look like round peas, but with an unmistakable white heart-shaped spot. When ripened, the seeds have turned black and the hearts are more pronounced. Herbalists in the Middle Ages believed the plant was good medicine for heart disease.

This plant tends to bring out the child in each of us. Although these flowers are insignificant, its fruit is a soft pale green seed pod, or capsule, that looks like a three-angled balloon. The 1-inch inflated pod, which holds the seeds, is green and soft until it becomes light brown and papery in the fall, when the three seeds in the pod can be harvested.

John Tampion's *Dangerous Plants* reports that *Cardiospermum halicacabum* also has the common name "blister creeper" because its sap is a skin irritant. I found no other reference to this common name or the irritating sap in any of the other books I checked, but once read it would be hard not to mention the risk. I'm very allergic to poison ivy, but I've had no problem playing with and popping the balloons all summer.

Love-in-a-puff is a tropical woody perennial usually grown as an annual. Although it's native to tropical America (Zones 9–10), it has been naturalized in many parts of the world and is widely cultivated. Because it doesn't transplant well, love-in-a-puff should be planted in peat pots in mid-March. Germination will take 5 to 10 days. Set out the seedlings 12 inches apart in the middle of May.

While love-in-a-puff grows quickly and thrives in dry hot regions such as Texas and the southwest, almost any good garden soil is fine. A warm, well-drained sandy loam is best. There are tendrils on the ends of the flower sprays by which it climbs, and, with a light lattice trellis to grow on and some early guidance, love-in-a-puff can reach 10 to 12 feet.

cathedral bells

Cobaea scandens (ko-BEE-uh SKAN-denz)

The eighteen climbing shrubs in the genus *Cobaea* are a testimony to Bernardo Cobo (1572–1659), Spanish missionary and naturalist, who spent forty-five years in Mexico and Peru. He finished his ten-volume natural history of the New World around 1650.

Perhaps the common names of cathedral bells and monastery bells originated with Cobo for the violet bell-shaped flowers, which are similar in shape to the flowers of canterbury bells, *Campanula medium*. This vine is also called cup-and-saucer vine, Mexican ivy, violet ivy, purple-bell, and fairy lanterns. *Scandens* is from the Latin *scando*, "to climb." *Cobaea scandens* was introduced between 1787 and 1792, a white-flowered one followed in 1872, and another, with variegated leaves, in 1874. I have been unable to find any mention of this last one in current literature.

The flowers bloom singly on long, fleshy-looking red stems over a long period of time. Because many stages of development are present at the same time, there are many gradations of color in the blooms. At first the closed bud stands vertically on its stem, but it bends when the flower begins to open. The flowers are 2 inches long, either greenish-purple or white, with a green petal-like calyx underneath. The saucerlike calyx lasts a while after the petals have fallen. Flowers of the purple variety are green and unpleasant smelling until they begin to change to purple, when they give off a sweet honey aroma that attracts bees. The white variety 'Alba' has lovely smooth white flowers. It blooms well into the fall and stops blooming only with the first hard frost.

Cathedral bells, native to the mountains of Mexico, is a perennial in the tropics (Zones 9–10), but in the north, it is treated as an annual. With sun, rich soil, and plenty of water, it will quickly grow 20 to 30 feet. Because it needs a long growing season, start the seeds indoors in February or March. The seeds are flat; for quickest germination, about 15 days, sow them on their sides with the edge showing. The seedlings should be pinched back so that bushy plants can be set out in mid-May when they're about a foot high.

Although it grows rapidly, this vine never provides more than a light visual screen for a porch. Like the sweet pea, it has branched tendrils at the end of each compound leaf that move around seeking support. The tendril is straight until it makes contact with a support, at which point it begins its spiral coiling, one branch turning in one direction and the other in the opposite direction. This draws the plant closer to its support, while providing enough flexibility to withstand stormy weather.

Cobaea scandens is reported to grow well in Florida, the Gulf States, California, and the Pacific Northwest, though I've seen many healthy specimens in the New York metropolitan area. It is not bothered by insects or diseases.

scarlet runner bean

Phaseolus coccineus (fas-SEE-ol-us kok-SIN-ee-us)

The vivid scarlet runner bean *Phaseolus coccineus*, formerly known as *P. multiflorus*, makes a far more substantial meal than the nasturtium. The name comes from the Latin *phaselus*, which means "little boat," after a Greek word for a bean pod's fanciful resemblance to a boat. *Coccineus* means "scarlet-colored." It's a native of the American tropics. This genus includes the kidney bean, the green (or string) bean, and the lima bean. The scarlet runner bean was cultivated by Thomas Jefferson at Monticello in 1791 and is now grown around the world.

The scarlet runner bean is sometimes called the Spanish bean, but its common name "fire bean" best describes how it sets the garden ablaze with color as it twines clockwise to 8 feet in full sun. In June and July the flowers are clustered like everlasting peas on 12-inch stalks, 10 to 30 to a spike, attracting hummingbirds. There are white-flowered, pink-flowered, and red- and white-flowered varieties as well as tastier cultivars, but none is as beautiful as the scarlet runner bean.

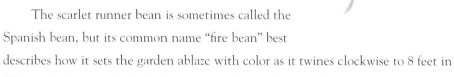

Common names for the white varieties are Dutch case-knife bean and Dutch runner.

Scarlet runner beans are very rapid-growing perennials cultivated as annuals in the north. Like most beans, they don't transplant well, and they need lots of sun and water, but the soil must be drained and moderately rich. They can be grown on teepees or trellises.

The edible beans are especially delicious when picked young—that is, when less than 3 inches long—and eaten raw or steamed. When very large, they are best boiled. While the flowers are a bright red, the fresh seeds are a spectacular scarlet, turning blue-black as they dry out and shrivel.

purple hyacinth bean
Lablab purpureus (LAB-lab pur-POO-ree-us)

The flamboyant purple hyacinth bean, also called lablab, Egyptian bean, Australian pea, Indian bean, or bonavista vine, has been written about frequently in the last few years. It's been mentioned throughout the century, however, and recently with the name *Dolichos lablab*. *Dolichos* comes from the Greek for "a form of pea," and *lablab* is from a Hindu plant name. It's usually said to be a native of Egypt, from which country it was introduced in 1818 according to Henderson, but at least one source gives its origin as India. *Hortus* only says it's probably from the Old World. Hyacinth bean is worth growing—at least once—for its huge seed pods, which are a most unusual, even shocking, shiny dark beet purple. There are both pink- and white-flowering varieties, but the white has green pods not nearly as interesting as the pink's purple pods. As the purple pods age, they begin to shrivel and turn more blue, until finally they become dry and brown.

Because the hyacinth bean is a big vine, you should plant it in front of a sturdy trellis or lattice wall. It twines clockwise and, with plenty of water, will quickly grow 15 to 20 feet in full sun. The compound leaves are purplish green and the stems and leaf stalks are purple. Hyacinth bean makes a good screen because it is dense from the ground up.

The vine begins to flower as soon as it begins to climb. The flowers are borne on rigid stems that are 6 to 8 inches long and stand out from the plant. They look like sweet peas and last well when cut. By mid-summer the entire plant will be covered with the flowers, followed shortly by the amazing pods.

Like other legumes, hyacinth bean fixes nitrogen from the atmosphere and does not need a rich soil. It's a perennial in Zones 9–10 and needs a long, warm growing season—it thrives on heat and humidity, and the first frost will kill it. In the north, start hyacinth beans in peat pots in March, or about six weeks before the last frost, in moist, but not wet, soil. If the soil is too wet, the beans will rot. Plant the seeds with the "eye" facing down; they should sprout in a week or two. Plant the seedlings outside, spaced about a foot apart, after all risk of frost has passed. No insects or diseases plague the purple hyacinth bean.

In the United States, hyacinth beans are not grown to be eaten, but with special preparation to rid them of bitterness and toxic qualities they are a rich source of protein. Both seeds and pods are grown for food in Africa and Asia.

Elizabeth Lawrence, a writer from North Carolina, noted that the hyacinth bean has been called "Cuban vine" and also "Jack bean" after Jack and his beanstalk. And I would like to add a name that popped up in my family. After seeing a bowl of harvested seeds, my son called them "Oreo cookies" for their similarity to the "double-stuffed" classic.

black-eyed susan vine

Thunbergia alata (thun-BER-jee-uh ah-LAH-ta)

The black-eyed Susan, or Susie, vine, *Thunbergia alata*, is one of the easiest vines to grow. *Thunbergia* is named for Dr. Carl Pieter Thunberg (1743–1828), a Swedish physician and botanist and author of *Flora Japonica* (1784). Among the many plants that he described was the barberry, *Berberis thunbergii*. *Alata*, from the Latin, means "winged," for the winged petioles that make this an easy plant to identify.

The flowers are orange, yellow, or white; the centers are usually purplish black, but white or cream centers also occur. They bloom from July until the frost in a sunny location with rich, preferably moist soil. The leaves are toothed and somewhat triangular, like serrated arrowheads.

The black-eyed Susan vine is a perennial in Zones 10–11 and will flower in its first year when grown from seed. Originally from southern tropical Africa, it will be damaged by the slightest frost. It twines clockwise and usually grows about 5 feet, although I have seen an 8-foot chain-link fence in my city neighborhood garden festooned with black-eyed Susan flowers. This vine is often recommended for baskets because if not encouraged otherwise it grows downward.

For early flowers, sow seeds indoors 4 to 6 weeks before the last frost is due, gradually hardening off the plants before exposing them to the slightest touch of frost. Black-eyed Susan vine can easily be propagated from cuttings. If red spider mites get to the plant, spray it forcefully with water.

building a trellis

triptych

7 1/2" vertical

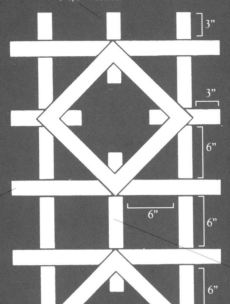

3"

3"

6"

HORIZONTALS:
6 at 22 1/2"
6 at 7 1/2"

6"

6"

2 at 15"
middle verticals

6"

3 squares
12 at 12"

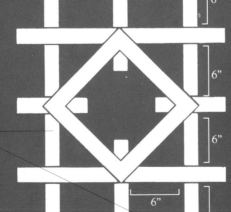

6"

6"

VERTICALS:
2 at 72"

6"

6"

12" vertical

7 1/2"

building a trellis

The trellis is a simple vertical design on which to contrast a beautiful vine. If the plant doesn't grow well—grows too slowly, or doesn't bloom, or gets cut down by an errant lawnmower—then the trellis is still there to provide some pleasant architecture for the garden. The trellis should have an appealing design because, for most of the year, especially in the north, it is all you see.

In my area there are interesting rustic trellises, some made out of cedar and others made out of grapevines, but I prefer the right angles and geometry of a grid. While I collected designs from old garden books and drove around upstate New York, I realized that I'd never use a week's paycheck to buy a trellis when I could build one myself.

I built my first trellis for less than ten dollars, the price of a cheap lunch in New York City. It was a simple grid made out of furring strips with 6-inch squares. Climbing nasturtiums quickly covered it. The trellis was so easy and inexpensive to build that I've had to resist the temptation to turn my yard into a miniature golf and trellis park.

If I can do it, you can do it. Building a trellis is no harder than cooking dinner. I happen to find cooking dinner quite difficult, mostly because I'm reluctant to do it. Once I give in to necessity and put aside a little time, I can do almost anything. Most household jobs are not that difficult. Painting a room is easy—the hard part is clearing the room, vacuuming the corners, and deciding on the color. The painting doesn't take long. So, like a pasta dinner with pesto, green salad, and hot rolls—a simple meal my sister makes to perfection—building a trellis is easy.

Choose a trellis design that is suitable with the design of your house. From 1924, Alfred C. Hottes advises in *A Little Book of Climbing Plants:*

In building trellis work in places where it is needed, avoid crossing the wooden strips so that they are proportioned like a ladder. Oftentimes one sees a home so ornamented with trellis work that it appears as if ladders had been allowed to remain at the sides of the buildings by painters or housebreakers. By adjusting the spacing of the strips this may be avoided. Simple trellis work, if well designed, is preferable to a complicated and ill-conceived pattern.

To build a trellis you need 1 × 2 stock, either rough cut or #2, from the lumber yard. Rough-cut wood is smooth on one side and rough on the other, and #2 is smooth on both sides. Remember that 1 × 2 is the nominal width in inches; the actual dimensions are smaller than 1 inch by 2 inches. In fact, they are ³⁄₄ inch by 1¹⁄₂ inches, perfect for a trellis. All of my diagrams are based on this proportion, and the width of the wood facing you is the 1¹⁄₂-inch face. For most of the designs you can buy 6-foot lengths of lumber because that is the maximum needed. If, however, you want a larger trellis, you can use the same designs and buy actual 2-inch-wide 8-foot lengths of wood. It is not a standard, readily available width, but some lumber yards will cut the wood for you, if you specify you want the actual width (not the nominal width) to be 2 inches.

My trellises are made of #2 white pine, and I painted them with an outdoor latex paint. Because I bring my large trellis into a barn for the winter, I have been able to use it for years without needing to repaint it. Pine is relatively inexpensive, as are spruce and fir. Different areas of the country will have different woods, but soft woods are always the most available and least expensive and are much easier to work with. For a more durable trellis, you have a choice of rot-resistant woods, such as black locust, cedar, redwood, and white oak. They can weather naturally or you can stain them for extra weather-proofing.

box kite

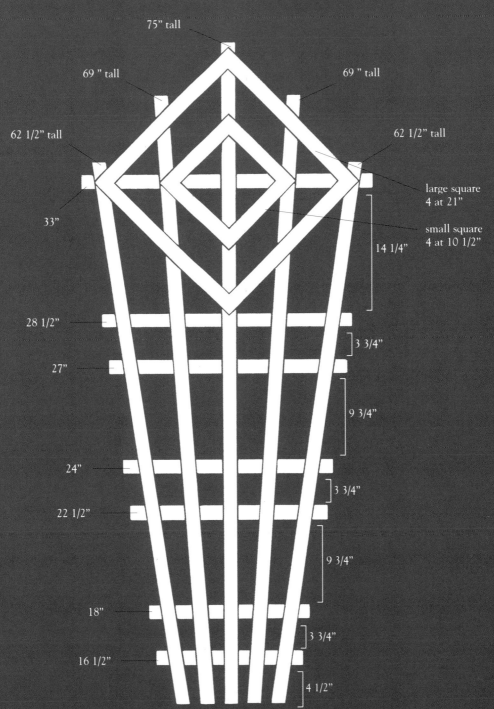

75" tall

69 " tall

69 " tall

62 1/2" tall

62 1/2" tall

33"

large square
4 at 21"

small square
4 at 10 1/2"

14 1/4"

28 1/2"

3 3/4"

27"

9 3/4"

24"

3 3/4"

22 1/2"

9 3/4"

18"

3 3/4"

16 1/2"

4 1/2"

pickets

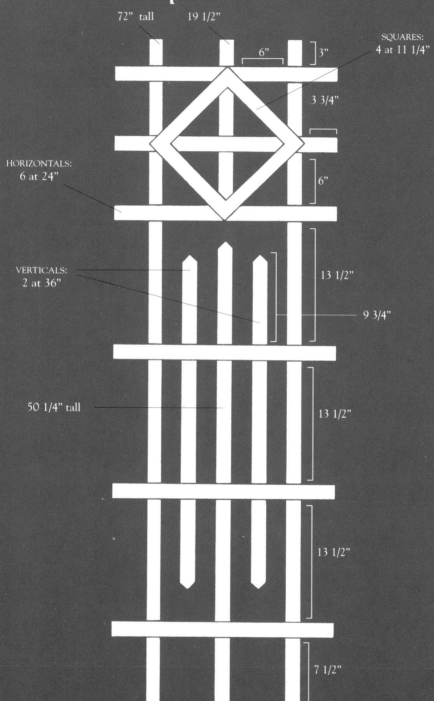

72" tall

19 1/2"

6"

3"

SQUARES:
4 at 11 1/4"

3 3/4"

HORIZONTALS:
6 at 24"

6"

VERTICALS:
2 at 36"

13 1/2"

9 3/4"

50 1/4" tall

13 1/2"

13 1/2"

7 1/2"

catwalk

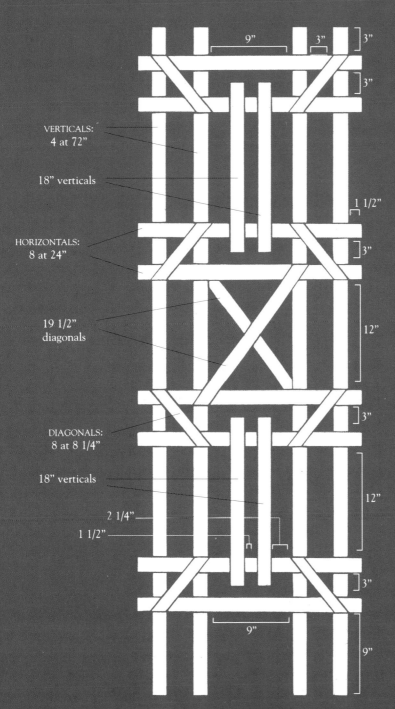

9" 3" 3"

3"

VERTICALS:
4 at 72"

18" verticals

1 1/2"

HORIZONTALS:
8 at 24"

3"

19 1/2"
diagonals

12"

DIAGONALS:
8 at 8 1/4"

3"

18" verticals

12"

2 1/4"

1 1/2"

3"

9"

9"

japanese fan

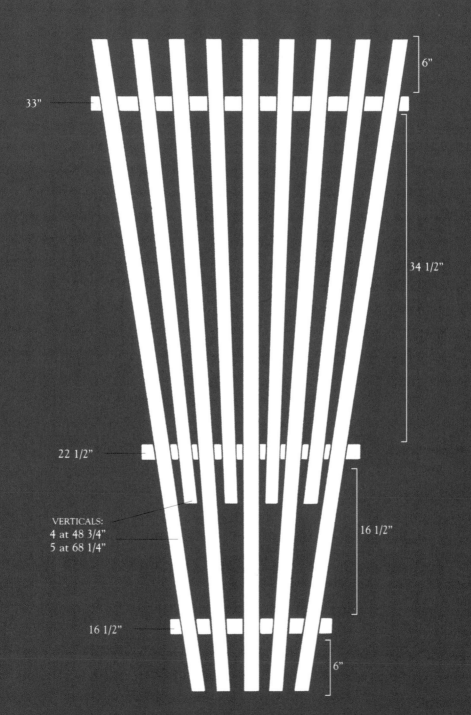

6"

33"

34 1/2"

22 1/2"

VERTICALS:
4 at 48 3/4"
5 at 68 1/4"

16 1/2"

16 1/2"

6"

Although I used pine 1 × 2s for the vertical uprights, I bought $\frac{1}{2}$-inch by 1$\frac{5}{8}$-inch pine molding (which actually measures $\frac{1}{2}$ inch by 1$\frac{1}{2}$ inches) for the cross pieces and the small pieces at the top of the vertical uprights. Although you pay more for less wood, you are buying better wood. Usually used for indoor trim, pine molding has no knots or imperfections and is finished (smooth) on all four sides, so the lines on the top pieces of the trellis are cleaner.

Curved pieces in the trellis designs are tricky to build. Cut a circle out of $\frac{1}{2}$-inch plywood. If you drill a hole first, you can insert a pointed compass or keyhole saw and easily cut a circle. Cut the smaller circle first so that it's easy to handle the wood when you cut the next, larger circle. A more expensive option is to buy extension jambs for arched windows.

You will need a few dozen galvanized steel screws to put the trellis together. To determine the number of screws you will need, count the number of intersections in your design and add a few extra for the ones that inevitably get lost. Screws are better than nails because they prevent the wood from splitting, and they hold the trellis together better when the wood shrinks and swells out there in the garden. You need galvanized screws so that they won't rust. If you are using 1 × 2 lumber, you will need 1-inch screws.

A handsaw is easy to use to cut the narrow strips of wood to make a trellis. If you need to buy a saw, buy a backsaw, a fine-toothed saw with a reinforced back—it will make a cleaner cut than will a saw with fewer and bigger teeth. To prevent the wood from splitting, drill pilot holes for the screws using a bit a little narrower than the shank of the screw. An electric drill with variable speed is easy to control, and, if you then use it with a driver point and Phillips-head screws, assembly is quick. A miter box, which guides the saw as you cut various fixed angles, would be handy, especially if you are making one of the more complicated trellises, but you can probably do without it. Just draw the lines and saw carefully.

You may decide to put your trellis out in the garden, but I always choose to place it either in front of or hanging on a wall. Remember to leave a 4- to 6-inch space behind the trellis so air can circulate to keep both the plant healthy and the wall dry. You will need to be able to remove the trellis occasionally to paint or repair the structure behind it.

There are several ways to hang a trellis. Which method you choose depends on where you plan to put the trellis and what you plan to grow on it. Remember always to use galvanized fastenings to prevent rust. You can fasten the trellis directly to the wall using lag bolts; use two at the top and two at the bottom, and don't forget to use wood spacing blocks between the trellis and the wall to maintain circulation. If your roof has an overhang (the old outhouse where I have mounted two trellises has one), you may be able to screw large hooks into the underside of it and hang the top of the trellis from them. You can set the bottom of the trellis in the ground. Dig holes for the supporting posts, at least 18 inches below ground level for a light trellis and 24 to 30 inches deep for a heavier one. Put stones or gravel in the bottom of each hole for drainage, set the posts, backfill with soil, and pack firmly. Remember to treat any wood you plan to bury with wood preservative. A more durable solution is to set the support posts on concrete piers—you can find instructions in landscaping and building how-to books. If you want to be able to remove the trellis from the wall without disturbing the perennial vine growing on it, you can set a hinged trellis on a permanent base. Use hooks and eyes at the top to hold the trellis to the wall and hinges near the bottom so that the trellis can be folded down away from the wall with the vine still attached.

Although it takes less than an hour to assemble a trellis, you may want to allow several days for the job. Figuring out how much and what kind of wood you need requires some focus. On another day you have to go to the lumber yard. Buying the

pagoda

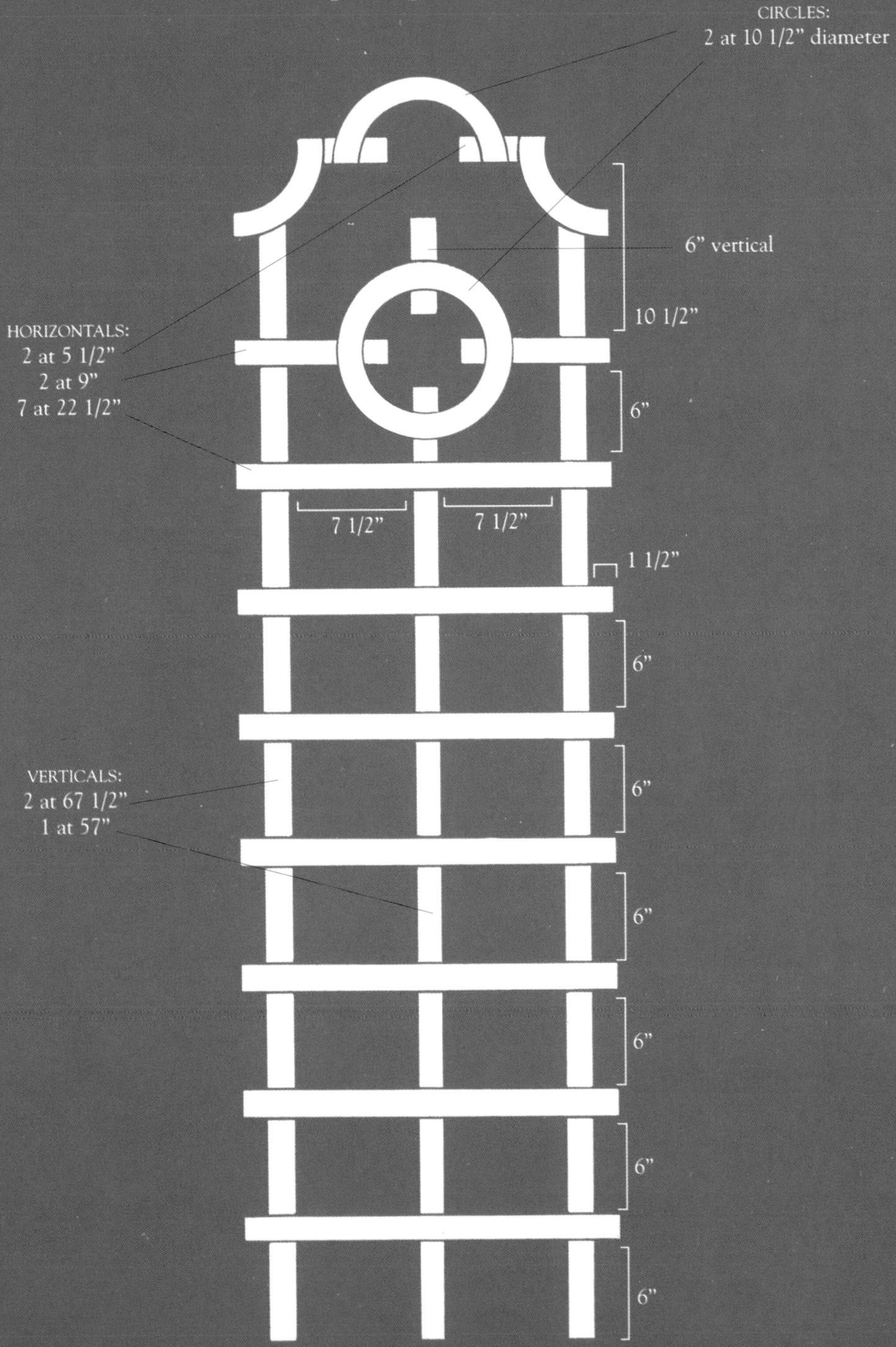

CIRCLES:
2 at 10 1/2" diameter

6" vertical

10 1/2"

HORIZONTALS:
2 at 5 1/2"
2 at 9"
7 at 22 1/2"

6"

7 1/2"   7 1/2"

1 1/2"

6"

6"

VERTICALS:
2 at 67 1/2"
1 at 57"

6"

6"

6"

6"

beacon

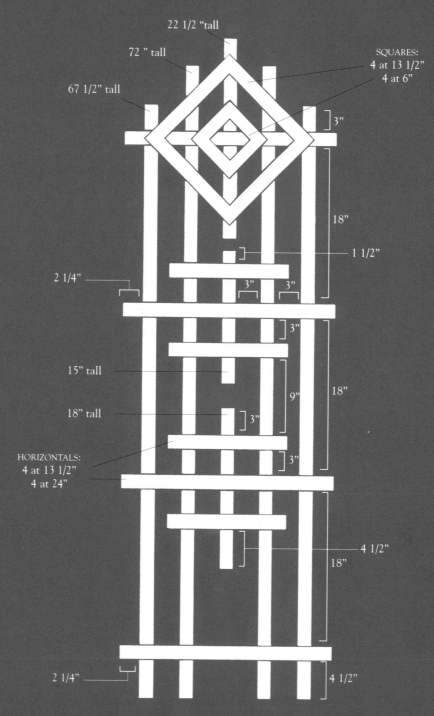

22 1/2 "tall

72 " tall

67 1/2" tall

SQUARES:
4 at 13 1/2"
4 at 6"

3"

18"

1 1/2"

2 1/4"

3"   3"

3"

15" tall

9"   18"

18" tall

3"

HORIZONTALS:
4 at 13 1/2"
4 at 24"

3"

4 1/2"

18"

2 1/4"

4 1/2"

sundial

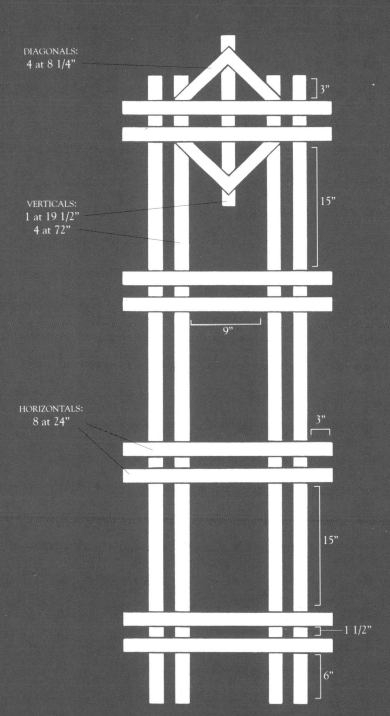

DIAGONALS:
4 at 8 1/4"

3"

VERTICALS:
1 at 19 1/2"
4 at 72"

15"

9"

HORIZONTALS:
8 at 24"

3"

15"

1 1/2"

6"

double diamond

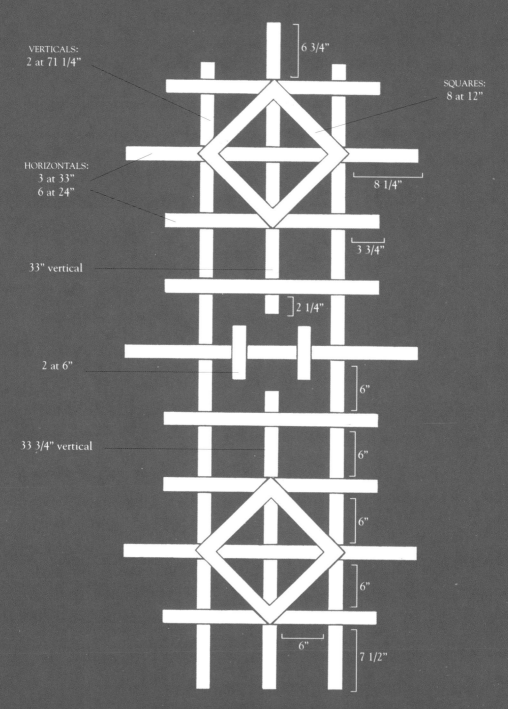

VERTICALS:
2 at 71 1/4"

6 3/4"

SQUARES:
8 at 12"

HORIZONTALS:
3 at 33"
6 at 24"

8 1/4"

3 3/4"

33" vertical

2 1/4"

2 at 6"

6"

33 3/4" vertical

6"

6"

6"

6"

7 1/2"

wood is enough for that day. Before you cut it, you might want to paint the wood—if you're painting or staining it—because it's faster to do all the wood together, but don't forget to apply paintable wood preservative to the posts before you paint if you plan to sink them in the ground. That's enough for that day. Cutting the pieces to size takes time and concentration, and once you've done it you'll want to screw everything together right away. After you've assembled the trellis, apply another coat of paint to seal the end grain exposed by your saw cuts and to seal around and hide the screw heads. Now, stand back and admire your work.

If you just can't bear to build a trellis yourself, there are plenty of ready-made trellises on the market, or there might be a good carpenter nearby. Our friend Joe built us some beautiful cabinets, and if I hadn't just made a trellis myself, I'd call Joe.

MATERIALS: rough-cut or #2 lumber

TOOLS AND SUPPLIES: backsaw

         compass or keyhole saw (for cutting circles)

         miter box (optional)

         drill, preferably electric with pilot bit and variable
           speed, or a hand drill and a screwdriver

         1″ galvanized Phillips-head screws

         galvanized steel hooks or lag bolts

         latex outdoor paint or wood stain

         oil-based paint or preservative for below-ground wood

         gravel or ready-mix concrete for subsurface piers

         paintbrush

epilogue

epilogue

New Year's Day, 1996. After spending most of my gardening years growing perennials, I have to admit that the evergreens and annual vines have been the most rewarding plantings. The evergreens provide privacy and structure, and the annuals offer a lot of color by the middle of summer and last well into autumn. The fall clean-up is easy when it's a matter of ripping out the annuals, instead of pruning them, and I like collecting the ripened seeds for the following year.

For the first time in years, however, the deer have eaten most of my winter garden, including a large daphne I planted eight years ago. The yews are threadbare, the juniper hedge has been reduced to a knee-high screen, and the mountain laurels and rhododendrons are without leaves. In the garden, it's one battle after another. Now it's deer eating the evergreens. Last spring it was a woodchuck eating the morning glories.

This woodchuck had a taste for morning glories and took up residence in the foundation under the porch. A dog is supposed to be some help with creatures lurking about the house, but Stella, who may or may not growl when a cat is nearby, only rolls her eyes when mice crisscross the kitchen. She was very interested in the woodchuck, though, and would go to the top of the cellar stairs where the draft carrying its perfume was strongest, throw back her head, and breathe deeply. While Stella inhaled, the woodchuck ate the morning glories I brought from Japan. (If woodchucks prefer broccoli, why did this one eat my vines?) I caught the offending woodchuck, which my friend Suzanne let me return in the borrowed trap, and planted out a few remaining seedlings that were growing in my makeshift greenhouses—old aquariums from the thrift shop—still in the house. Last summer the vines were beautiful after all.

Now I'm waiting again for spring. In the meantime, a few of my warm climate vines are thriving indoors. The evergreen Carolina jessamine *Gelsemium sempervirens* 'Pride of Augusta' transports me south with its fragrant double yellow blossoms. Out the window I can see lots of snow and the trellises—small pieces of architecture marking the location of the garden and reminding me of the pleasures to come.

invasive plants

One warning before you begin to experiment with vines. A list of "Invasive Nonindigenous Plants" compiled by the Exotic Pest Plant Council (EPPC) warns against invasive plants that outcompete native vegetation. Even if your favorite nursery, or your best friend, offers an interesting vine, it may not be suitable for your area. In fact, some vines, like ampelopsis, are so invasive and such a threat to the natural vegetation that their cultivation is discouraged by local regulation. The EPPC recommends against using some of the plants in this book in "low-maintenance sites close to natural areas, such as roadsides and second homes." Since I'm in the garden only on weekends, I feel the finger pointed at me.

Ampelopsis brevipedunculata is a problem in the area around New York City. I've seen backyards and gardens draped with so many plants that it's not possible to weed out all of the seedlings. When my plant threatened to take over, I replaced it with a smaller cultivar with variegated leaves called 'Elegans,' and it suits me just fine. Not only does 'Elegans' grow half as tall, it grows more slowly so that you will have time to weed out any unwanted seedlings spread by the birds. But if you live in the Rockies, where the vine is not considered invasive, maybe you can give the species a try. It's beautiful—just beware.

For more information write to the EPPC Government Liaison, 8208 Dabney Avenue, Springfield, Virginia 22153. Here are the plants on their list that appear in this book:

BOTANICAL NAME	COMMON NAME	REPORTED INVASIVE IN
Akebia quinata	five-leaf akebia	Alabama, Virginia
Ampelopsis brevipedunculata	porcelain berry	Maryland, New York, Virginia, and the Northeast
Cardiospermum halicacabum	love-in-a-puff	Arkansas, Virginia
Euonymus fortunei	climbing euonymus	Alabama, Illinois, Maryland, Missouri, Virginia, potentially Delaware, Pennsylvania
Lonicera periclymenum	woodbine	Connecticut, Delaware, Kentucky, Maine, Massachusetts, Michigan, Minnesota, New Hampshire, New Jersey, New York, North Carolina, Pennsylvania, Rhode Island, Tennessee, Vermont, Virginia, West Virginia, Wisconsin

I do *not* recommend either Japanese honeysuckle (*Lonicera japonica*) or Chinese wisteria (*Wisteria sinensis*), because they cause problems in many states. Both are invasive across wide areas of the Mid-Atlantic, Southeast, South, Northeast, and Appalachian and Plains states.

sources of plants, seeds,
and ready-made trellises

THE ANTIQUE ROSE EMPORIUM
Route 5, Box 143
Brenham, TX 77833
(800) 441-0002
Roses

APPALACHIAN GARDENS
P. O. Box 82
Waynesboro, PA 17268-0082
(717) 762-4312
Some vines

AUTUMN GLADE BOTANICALS
46857 W. Ann Arbor Trail
Plymouth, MI 48170
(313) 459-2604 FAX
Tropaeolum speciosum

**THE COMPLEAT GARDEN
CLEMATIS NURSERY**
217 Argilla Road
Ipswich, MA 01938-2617
(508) 356-3197
Clematis

COUNTRY BLOOMERS NURSERY
R. R. 2
Udall, KS 67146
(316) 986-5518
Old and miniature roses

FOREST FARM
990 Tetherow Road
Williams, OR 97544-9599
(541) 846-7269
Good variety of vines

D.S. GEORGE NURSERIES
2515 Penfield Road
Fairport, NY 14450
(716) 377-0731
Clematis

GILSON GARDENS INC.
3059 U. S. Route 20
P. O. Box 277
Perry, OH 44081
(216) 259-5252
Some vines

GIRARD NURSERIES
6839 North Ridge East
P. O. Box 428
Geneva, OH 44041
(216) 466-2881
Some vines

GREER GARDENS
1280 Goodpasture Island Road
Eugene, OR 97401-1794
(800) 548-0111
Many vines

HERONSWOOD NURSERY LTD
7530 N.E. 288th Street
Kingston, WA 98346-9502
(360) 297-4172
Some vines

KARTUZ GREENHOUSES
1408 Sunset Drive
Vista, CA 92083-6531
(619) 941-3613
Tropical and subtropical vines

LAMB NURSERIES
Route 1, Box 460B
Long Beach, WA 98631
(360) 642-4856
Some vines

LOGEE'S GREENHOUSES
141 North Street
Danielson, CT 06239
(203) 774-8038
Tropical vines

LOUISIANA NURSERY
Route 7, Box 43
Opelousas, LA 70570
(318) 948-3696
Many vines

MELLINGER'S INC.
2310 W. South Range Road
North Lima, OH 44452-9731
(216) 549-9861
Many vines

MERRY GARDENS
Camden, ME 04843
(207) 236-9064
Many tropical vines

MILAEGER'S GARDENS
4838 Douglas Avenue
Racine, WI 53402-2498
(800) 669-9956
Many vines

MILLER NURSERIES
5060 West Lake Road
Canandaigua, NY 14424
(800) 836-9630
Trellises and some vines

NICHE GARDENS
1111 Dawson Road
Chapel Hill, NC 27516
(919) 967-0078
Some vines

NOR'EAST MINIATURE ROSES, INC.
P. O. Box 307
Rowley, MA 01969
(508) 948-7964
Miniature roses

OREGON MINIATURE ROSES, INC.
8285 S.W. 185th Avenue
Beaverton, OR 97007-6712
(503) 649-4482
Miniature roses

THE ROSERAIE AT BAYFIELDS
P. O. Box R
Waldoboro, ME 04572
(207) 832-6330
Roses

ROSES OF YESTERDAY AND TODAY
803 Brown's Valley Road
Watsonville, CA 95076-0398
(408) 724-3537
Roses

ROSLYN NURSERY
211 Burrs Lane
Dix Hills, NY 11746
(516) 643-9347
Many vines

WAYSIDE GARDENS
1 Garden Lane
Hodges, SC 29695-0001
(800) 845-1124
Trellises and many vines

WHITE FLOWER FARM
Route 63
Litchfield, CT 06759-0050
(800) 503-9624
Some vines

WOODLANDERS, INC.
1128 Colleton Avenue
Aiken, SC 29801
(803) 648-7522
Many vines

Seeds

ABUNDANT LIFE SEED FOUNDATION
P. O. Box 772/1029 Lawrence Street
Port Townsend, WA 98368
(206) 385-5660

W. ATLEE BURPEE & CO.
300 Park Avenue
Warminster, PA 18991-0001
(800) 888-1447

THE COOK'S GARDEN
P. O. Box 535
Londonderry, VT 05148-0535
(802) 824-3400

**FOX HOLLOW HERB AND
HEIRLOOM SEED CO.**
P. O. Box 148
McGrann, PA 16236
(412) 548-SEED

THE FRAGRANT PATH
P. O. Box 328
Fort Calhoun, NE 68023

J.L. HUDSON, SEEDSMAN
P. O. Box 1058
Redwood City, CA 94064

NWN NURSERY
1365 Watford Circle
Chipley, FL 32428
(904) 638-7572
Seeds and plants

PINETREE GARDEN SEEDS
Box 300
New Gloucester, ME 04260
(207) 926-3400

SELECT SEEDS ANTIQUE FLOWERS
180 Stickney Road
Union, CT 06076-4617
(203) 684-9310

SHEPHERD'S GARDEN SEEDS
30 Irene Street
Torrington, CT 06790
(860) 482-3638
Flowering vines collection
Biomesh trellises

THOMPSON AND MORGAN
P. O. Box 1308
Jackson, NJ 08527-0308
(800) 274-7333
Mostly seeds, some plants

Trellises and Supplies

GARDEN ARCHITECTURE
631 North Third Street
Philadelphia, PA 19123
(215) 545-5442
Cedar trellises

GARDENERS EDEN
P. O. Box 7307
San Francisco, CA 94120-7307
(800) 822-9600
Tools and supplies

GARDENER'S SUPPLY COMPANY
128 Intervale Road
Burlington, VT 05401-2804
(802) 863-1700
Trellises and tools

M. R. LABBE, CO.
P. O. Box 467
Biddeford, ME 04005
(207) 282-3420
Red cedar arbors and trellises

A. M. LEONARD, INC.
241 Fox Drive
P. O. Box 816
Piqua, OH 45356
(800) 543-8955
Tools and supplies

LANGENBACH
Dept. L62100
P. O. Box 1420
Lawndale, CA 90260-6320
(800) 362-1991
Trellises and tools

NEW ENGLAND GARDEN ORNAMENTS
P. O. Box 431
38 East Brookfield Road
North Brookfield, MA 01535-0431
(508) 867-4474
Metal and mahogany trellises and arbors

THE PAINTED GARDEN, INC.
304 Edge Hill Road
Glenside, PA 19038
(215) 884-7378
Metal trellises

SMITH & HAWKEN
Two Arbor Lane, Box 6900
Florence, KY 41022-6900
(800) 776-3336
Trellises and tools

TAYLOR RIDGE FARM
P. O. Box 222
Saluda, NC 28773
(704) 749-4756
Steel and copper trellises

WALPOLE WOODWORKERS
424 Ethan Allen Highway
P. O. Box 535
Ridgefield, CT 06877
(203) 438-3134
Big cedar panels

WOOD INNOVATIONS OF SUFFOLK
P. O. Box 356
265 Middle Island Road
Medford, NY 11763
(516) 698-2345
Cedar trellises

bibliography

S. Arnott, *The Book of Climbing Plants and Wall Shrubs*, London: John Lane, The Bodley Head, 1903

L.H. Bailey, *The Gardener's Handbook*, NY: The Macmillan Company, 1943

Neltje Blanchan, *The American Flower Garden*, NY: Doubleday, Page & Company, 1913

Caroline Boisset, *The Plant Growth Planner*, NY: Prentice Hall, 1992

———, *Vertical Gardening*, NY: Weidenfeld and Nicolson, 1988

Bernice Brilmayer, *All about Vines and Hanging Plants*, Garden City, NY: Doubleday & Company Inc., 1962

Alice Coats, *Garden Shrubs and their Histories*, NY: E.P. Dutton and Company, Inc, 1964

———, *The Plant Hunters*, NY: McGraw-Hill Book Co., 1969

Barbara Crandall and Chuck Crandall, *Flowering, Fruiting and Foliage Vines*, NY: Sterling Publishing Co., 1995

Charles Darwin, *Climbing Plants*, NY: D. Appleton & Co., 1893

Michael A. Dirr, *Manual of Woody Landscape Plants*, Champaign, IL: Stipes Publishing Company, 1990

Florence DuCane, *The Flowers and Gardens of Japan*, London: A.& C. Black, 1908

Alice Morse Earle, *Old Time Gardens*, NY: The Macmillan Company, 1901

Richard Folkard Jr., *Plant Lore, Legends and Lyrics*, London: S. Low, Marston, Searle, and Rivington, 1884

Helen M. Fox, *Gardening with Herbs*, NY: The Macmillan Company, 1933

Barry Fretwell, *Clematis*, Deer Park, WI: Capability's Books, 1989

Hilderic Friend, *Flowers and Flower Lore*, London: S. Sonnenschein, Le Bas Lowrey, 1886

Mark Griffiths and J.K. Burras, Ed., *Manual of Climbers and Wall Plants*, Portland, OR: Timber Press, 1994

Peter Henderson, *Peter Henderson's Handbook of Plants*, NY: Peter Henderson & Company, 1881

Alfred C. Hottes, *A Little Book of Climbing Plants*, NY: A. T. De La Mare Company, Inc., 1933

Frances Howard, *Landscaping with Vines*, NY: The Macmillan Company, 1959

Alphonse Karr, *A Tour Round My Garden*, London: Routledge, Warne, & Routledge, 1859

G.W. Kerr, *Sweet Peas Up-to-Date*, Philadelphia: W. Atlee Burpee & Co., 1910

Allen Lacy, *Gardening with Groundcovers and Vines*, NY: HarperCollins Publishers, 1993

Elizabeth Lawrence, *Gardening for Love: The Market Bulletins*, Durham: Duke University Press, 1987

———, (ed. by William Neal), *Through the Garden Gate*, Chapel Hill: The University of North Carolina Press, 1990

Christopher Lloyd, *Clematis*, London: Collins, 1977

Alice Lounsberry, *Southern Wildflowers & Trees*, NY: Frederick A. Stokes Company Publishers, 1901

Ernest Markham, *Clematis,* NY: Charles
    Scribner's Sons, 1935

William C. McCollom, *Vines and How to
    Grow Them,* Garden City, NY: Doubleday,
    Page & Company, 1911

William C. Mulligan, *The Lattice Gardener,*
    NY: Macmillan, 1995

Beverley Nichols, *Garden Open Tomorrow,*
    London: William Heinemann Ltd., 1968

Harold O. Perkins, *Espaliers and Vines
    for the Home Gardener,* Princeton, NJ: D. Van
    Nostrand Company, Inc., 1964

Frances Perry, *Flowers of the World,* NY: The
    Hamlyn Publishing Group, 1972

Vernon Quinn, *Stories and Legends of Garden
    Flowers,* NY: F. A. Stokes, 1939

Lee Reich, *Uncommon Fruits Worthy of Attention,*
    Reading, MA: Addison-Wesley Publishing
    Company, Inc., 1991

Betty W. Richards and Anne Kaneko,
    Japanese Plants: Know Them & Use Them,
    Tokyo: Shufunotomo Co., Ltd., 1991

Stephen Scanniello and Tania Bayard,
    Climbing Roses, NY: Prentice Hall, 1994

Stephen A. Spongberg, *A Reunion of Trees,*
    Cambridge, MA: Harvard University
    Press, 1990

John Tampion, *Dangerous Plants,* NY:
    Universe Books, 1977

Jane Taylor, *Climbers and Wall Plants for
    Year Round Colour,* London: Ward Lock
    Limited, 1993

Cordelia Harris Turner, *The Floral Kingdom,
    Its History, Sentiment and Poetry,* Chicago:
    Moses Warren, c. 1876

Nancy J. Turner and Adam F. Szczawinski,
    *Common Poisonous Plants and Mushrooms
    of North America,* Portland, OR: Timber
    Press, 1991

Michael Tyler-Whittle and Christopher
    Cook, *Curtis's Flower Garden Displayed,*
    Leicester, England: Magna Books, 1991

Michael Tyler-Whittle, *The Plant Hunters,*
    NY: PAJ Publications, 1988

Charles W. J. Unwin, *Sweet Peas: Their
    History, Development, Culture,* NY: D.
    Appleton and Co., 1926

Yoshitaka Watanabe, *The Japanese Morning
    Glory,* Tokyo: Nihon Terebi, Showa, 1984

Clarence Moores Weed, *The Flower
    Beautiful,* Boston: Houghton, Mifflin and
    Company, 1903

Lyman N. White, *Heirlooms and Genetics,*
    Cambridge, NY: Lyman N. White
    Publisher, 1981

Louise Beebe Wilder, *Colour in My Garden,*
    Garden City, NY: Doubleday, Doran &
    Company, Inc., 1930

Ernest H. Wilson, *Aristocrats of the Garden,*
    NY: Doubleday, Page & Company, 1917

Wayne Winterrowd, *Annuals for Connoisseurs,*
    NY: Prentice Hall, 1992

Wonderful Wooden Garden Structures,
    (previously published as *Beautifying the
    Home Grounds*), Hillsborough, NC:
    Hummer Press, 1992

Richardson Wright, *Greedy Gardeners,*
    NY: J.B. Lippincott Company, 1955

Donald Wyman, *Shrubs and Vines for
    American Gardens,* NY: The Macmillan
    Company, 1969

acknowledgments

My friends and family are wonderful—they've helped with every aspect of this book. They've grown vines, saved seeds, taken photographs, and recommended plants. I'd especially like to thank: Bobbi Angell, for sending photographs of vines that weren't growing in my garden; Suzanne Borris, for taking home the woodchuck that lived under my porch; Emilie Fromm, for giving me a lot of trees, shrubs, and vines; Katy Gilmore, for writing to me about good vines for growing in Alaska; Lori Hogan, for calling me when the 'Silver Moon' rose was blooming; Brian Hotchkiss, for sending photographs of a beautiful clematis; Jane Hoffman and Mary Jenkins, for their interest in the project; Madeleine Keeve, for recommending many of the vines included here; Norma Kelly, for introducing me to 'Jeanne Lajoie'; Michael Longacre, for reporting on his collection of roof-top vines; Mary Lynch and Tessie Tuniman, for letting me grow vines on a fence near the New York University Blood Donor Center; Lee Reich, for letting me sketch in his garden; Joyce Robins, for loving the sweet potato vine 'Blackie'; Ellen Scordato, for her willingness to grow vines indoors; Joe and Nancy Smith, for their advice on carpentry and gardening; Michelle Strutin, for brainstorming about good vines to grow in the Rockies; Sandy Wilmot, for nurturing a sampler of annual vines in the north country; and Jody Winer, for helping me to write about all of this. And for his love of birds, I'd like to remember my late friend and co-worker Tim Allan, who also found peace in his garden.

Sarah and Vanessa Longacre have supported my many endeavors—not the least of which are trying to build trellises and to cook. My son, Isaac, checked my math and traveled with me to Japan. Sumiko and Norman Cook showed us gardens in Japan and translated every seed packet that struck my fancy. Sumiko also translated the Masa-oka Shiki poem on moonflowers. My husband, Ken Krabbenhoft, believed that I could and would write a garden book one day, and my father, Topper Cook, encouraged me to take on the project when I had the opportunity. My mother, Nancy Cook, has been one of my most ardent promoters all along.

Enthusiastic thanks go to all at Artisan—Leslie Stoker, Jim Wageman, Hope Koturo, Beth Wareham, Christina Sheldon, and Alexandra Maldonado—and to the designer Jennifer S. Hong. For other editorial and horticultural skills, I'm indebted to Jennie McGregor Bernard, Carole Berglie, and Mary Mantuani. Most of all, thanks to Ann ffolliott for supporting this book wholeheartedly.

index

DESIGNED BY JENNIFER S. HONG

TYPEFACES IN THIS BOOK ARE
GOUDY OLD STYLE, DESIGNED BY FREDERIC W. GOUDY,
AND BODEGA SERIF, DESIGNED BY GREG THOMPSON

PRINTED AND BOUND BY
IMAGO PRODUCTIONS (F.E.) PTE.
SINGAPORE